UNLOCKED

T.D. JAKES

UNLOCKED

STEP INTO YOUR
NEXT-LEVEL MOMENT

THE **KEY** TO YOUR **PROMOTION** AND **BLESSING**

Previously published content from *When Power Meets Potential*

DESTINY IMAGE® PUBLISHERS, INC.
P. O. Box 310, Shippensburg, PA 17257-0310
"Promoting Inspired Lives"

This book and all other Destiny Image and Destiny Image fiction books are available at Christian bookstores and distributors worldwide.

For more information on foreign distributors, call 717-532-3040.

Reach us on the Internet: www.destinyimage.com.

ISBN 13 TP: 978-0-7684-0810-2

ISBN 13 Ebook: 978-0-7684-0811-9

For Worldwide Distribution. Printed in the U.S.A.

1 2 3 4 5 6 7 8 / 18 17 16 1

CONTENTS

BONUS MATERIAL

INTRODUCTION

Life is full of destiny-defining moments. The question is: *How will you respond when yours come along?* Your response to these moments is what unlocks the potential inside of you and brings you closer to fulfilling your destiny in God.

In *Unlocked*, I want to give you some practical keys from the lives of the Old Testament prophets, Elijah and Elisha, that will help you identify the moments—seemingly ordinary and normal—that might just be God-designed catalysts that catapult you right into divine destiny.

Elijah represented Elisha's destiny-defining moment. Even though Elijah was a prophet and a person, he also personified the divine timing of Heaven that unlocked Elisha's potential and positioned him to fulfill his purpose. Elijah was a destiny-defining connection that called Elisha out from his old season and into the new.

Up until Elijah came onto the scene, Elisha did what he always knew to do. He lived in familiar surroundings. I'm sure he was comfortable with the way things had always been. Maybe he was even "top of the class" in that place, that time, and that season. In many ways, Elisha had gone to the ceiling of his former season. Maybe this describes you.

Maybe you feel like you're ready to break out of where you currently are—like what you have always known and done just can't hold you anymore. It was good for a season. Maybe even a long season. In fact, it was even God-ordained for a time! But remember, you serve the God who brings His people from glory to glory. He is not interested in you setting up a permanent residence in some former glory when He is summoning you into new heights, new depths, new anointing, new opportunities, new strategies, new contacts, new ideas, new wisdom, new wealth, new blessing, new favor, and new increase.

You are being called by the God of the new thing, who calls us to forget the former things; do not dwell on the past.

> *See, I am doing a new thing! Now it springs up; do you not perceive it?...* (Isaiah 43:19 NIV).

As we go on this journey together, I pray your eyes would be opened. I pray that you would start to clearly recognize and discern the moments, the connections, the relationships, and the catalysts that God has orchestrated in your life that are summoning you from one level to another, from one season into the next, and from one glory to another glory!

Something's stirring, isn't it? You feel like, somehow, you've outgrown where you've always been. Where you have been no longer satisfies and where you are going is bigger than you could ever have dreamed. Get ready to seize your moments and step through Heaven's open doors!

Just remember, it was through one casual exchange with the prophet Elijah that Elisha was granted the invitation to fulfill his destiny and change the landscape of his world. The same is true for you.

CHAPTER 1

RECOGNIZE YOUR MOMENT

And he left the oxen and ran after Elijah, and said, "Please let me kiss my father and my mother, and then I will follow you..." (1 Kings 19:20).

ARE YOU READY?

[Jesus said], *"No one, having put his hand to the plow, and looking back, is fit for the kingdom of God"* (Luke 9:62).

When Elijah shows up, everything changes. When our moment comes, we must be ready.

Elisha recognized his moment. He was ready. This is why God denies moments of power to those *before* their moment is ready. A moment that transitions you from one season to the next can actually be deadly if you are ill-prepared for the moment.

I want to help you get ready, so that when Elijah shows up, you recognize the arrival of the moment that changes everything. Because let me tell you, when that moment comes, you can't go back to who you were. You won't be able to. *When you catch a glimpse of what you have been called into, what you're being called out of will never satisfy you again.* To return to what you are being called out of would be living beneath what has become available. I believe God does everything in His power to make this type of regression impossible. Does it happen? Sadly, yes. But not to you. Don't let it happen to you. Be the one who embraces the journey. Go from glory to glory and strength to strength.

Look at Elisha's moment:

Elisha left the oxen standing there, ran after Elijah, and said to him, "First let me go and kiss my father and mother good-bye, and then I will go with you!" Elijah replied, "Go on back, but think about what I have done to you" (1 Kings 19:20 NLT).

Elisha was ready for his moment, absolutely. When he tells Elijah that he is going to go back and kiss his father and mother good-bye, he is not behaving like the example Jesus gives us in Luke 9:61, who says,

"Lord, I will follow You, but let me first go and bid them farewell who are at my house."

There are two different perspectives here. Let's contrast these two accounts for a moment. Elisha was ready for his next season, but still returned to his household, while the people in Luke's Gospel account are obviously *not* ready for their next season.

NO TURNING BACK

In Luke 9, Jesus gives examples of those who would be crushed by the cost of discipleship if they had continued on with Him while maintaining the attitudes and paradigms they demonstrated. Read what happened:

> *Now it happened as they journeyed on the road, that someone said to Him, "Lord, I will follow You wherever You go." And Jesus said to him, "Foxes have holes and birds of the air have nests, but the Son of Man has nowhere to lay His head." Then He said to another, "Follow Me." But he said, "Lord, let me first go and bury my father." Jesus said to him, "Let the dead bury their own dead, but you go and preach the kingdom of God." And another also said, "Lord, I will follow You, but let me first go and bid them farewell who are at my house." But Jesus said to him, "No one, having put his hand to the plow, and looking back,*

is fit for the kingdom of God" (Luke 9:57-62).

Even though the situations each of the people in Luke 9 discussed seemed valid—from the one who wanted to bury his father to the one who wanted to bid farewell to his household—context is what assigns meaning to what was taking place in this text. It was not a parable. It was not a story. It was reality.

Jesus was journeying on the road, and came across at least three different people who wanted to follow Him, but also wanted to go their own way. They wanted a mixture. It had little to do with just burying a father or saying good-bye to family members. Hearts were divided. They did not recognize the power that was passing them by, power that could unlock their potential and push them into their next seasons. Jesus had this power; sadly, the three examples we read about were ill-prepared for their moments of visitation.

Even though Jesus was asking them to make some significant sacrifices at the same time, He was inviting them to journey along the same road He was traveling. There is no greater fulfillment to the question, *What's my purpose in life?* than to be one who journeys alongside Jesus.

The Kingdom of God does not offer a two-for-one special.

The three individuals in Luke 9 wanted both Jesus *and* their way. The Kingdom of God does not offer a two-for-one special, where we get the best of God and the best of mediocrity. The best of the Kingdom and the best of the world. The best of the holy and the best of the vile. The best of the glory and the best of the profane. In fact, there is no room for God's best and second rate to take up residence together. They will not peacefully cohabitate. One will rule the day.

Our hearts don't have the capacity for dual-surrendering. We either yield to God, or we turn back and go our own way. Jesus recognized this and knew that these individuals did not recognize their moment. If they truly knew who was standing before them, inviting them into a lifestyle of journeying the same road as He, the attachments that they ended up listing would have been nonissues. Why? Because when potential recognizes its moment of power, it responds appropriately. This reveals the maturity level of the one carrying potential.

Excuses reveal immaturity. Remember, immaturity demonstrates that we will not hold up under the weight and pressure of promotion. Perfection is not required for promotion, but there is a degree of maturity that is required in order to sustain us during the period of transition into a new season. Jesus gives us three examples of immature people who had potential, but were not ready for their intersection with power.

WHAT'S ON THE OTHER SIDE?

Think about it. These three people in Luke 9 *could* have been disciples. They could have joined the ranks of those who turned the world upside down (see Acts 17:6). Their hands could have been used to heal the sick, diseased, leprous, and maligned. They could have been mouthpieces touched by the fiery words of Heaven to preach the piercing and powerful truth of the Gospel. They could have trampled upon all the works of the enemy (see Luke 10:19). They *could* have released their potential and gone down in history as those who were *"with Jesus"* (see Acts 4:13).

We have just reviewed what these people *could* have done with their potential. So what happened? They did not recognize their moment standing right before them. They did not have a vision for what was on the other side of Jesus' invitation.

I encourage you, be ready for your moment. There's nothing for you back there. You know where "back there" is. I'm not telling you to leave your family. I'm not asking you to go overseas. I'm not saying sell the dog, trade in the car for a jalopy, and completely rearrange your current living situation. Jesus was more focused on their hearts than He was the externals. Family is not bad. Attending funerals is not wrong. Rather, it's a divided heart that delivers the wrong answer when Jesus walks up and invites you to join Him on the journey.

> *A divided heart delivers the wrong answer when Jesus walks up and invites you to join Him on the journey.*

Be sure that your heart is undivided when Jesus reveals Himself. So many of us want the perks of God's power without the anchor of responsibility. This is not possible. For power to be released, and ultimately sustained, it requires a suitable resting place. In order for your potential to be released, you must be a willing and obedient vessel that God's power can touch and make demands of. Power knows better. Power is touching you because it knows where it can take you. However, power requires your cooperation. It will not drag you kicking and screaming, spitting and clawing. Power is looking for those who will say "Yes" to its invitation.

What could have happened to these would-be disciples along the road if they had responded to their moment? I believe Luke gives us a glimpse of what would have been possible for those who said "No" to Jesus because they wanted their next season on their terms. The concluding verses of Luke 9 transition seamlessly into Luke 10 where we are given a vision of what would have been available to the disciples who settled for second rate when power was beckoning them.

Let's briefly look through Luke 10:1-9:

> ***After these things*** *the Lord appointed seventy others also, and sent them two by two before His face into every city*

*and place where He Himself was about
to go* (Luke 10:1).

After *what* things? Jesus identified those
ready for their moment and positioned them
for their next season. It's amazing how quickly
this season was coming. Think about it. Those
who said "No" to Jesus's invitation said "No" to
a whole new way of living that was just around
the corner.

Those who recognized the cost and
responded to their moment were commissioned as the "seventy others" who become sent
ones. To become a "sent one," we must respond
appropriately to the moment standing before us.
Power stood before these disciples, ready and
eager to unlock their potential. Power would
not have even approached these individuals if
there was no potential.

In the same way, power wants to visit you.
Power wants to unlock what's inside you and
turn someone who was walking along the road

of life into an ambassador of another world, sent to proclaim the advancing Kingdom of God. Power takes ordinary plowers and turns them into anointed prophets.

We read on:

> *Then He said to them, "The harvest truly is great, but the laborers are few; therefore pray the Lord of the harvest to send out laborers into His harvest. Go your way; behold, I send you out as lambs among wolves. Carry neither money bag, knapsack, nor sandals; and greet no one along the road. But whatever house you enter, first say, 'Peace to this house.' And if a son of peace is there, your peace will rest on it; if not, it will return to you. And remain in the same house, eating and drinking such things as they give, for the laborer is worthy of his wages. Do not go from house to house. Whatever city you enter, and they receive you, eat such things as are set before you. And heal the sick there, and*

say to them, 'The kingdom of God has come near to you'" (Luke 10:2-9).

This was the lifestyle that Jesus was summoning people into; and ultimately, this is what they were saying "No" to. Jesus was calling forth laborers who would heal the sick, raise the dead, and destroy the works of the devil. He was commissioning disciples to step into their purpose as spokespeople for an eternal, unshakeable Kingdom.

Your response to power's invitation has enormous implications. If those walking along the road would have said "Yes" to Jesus, they would have been immediately launched into the Luke 10 lifestyle we just read about. Unfortunately, their moment walked right up to them and they were not ready.

Are you ready to be unlocked? I want you to be. That is why we are going through these stories. That's why we are looking at these lives. I want to overwhelm you with information and truth and revelation that position you to be on the ready line when your moment of power arrives.

ELISHA'S RESPONSE

On the other end, we notice Elisha's response to Elijah. At first glance, how Elisha reacts does not seem all that different from the would-be disciples of Luke 9. Look again, because it's all about context. The difference between Elisha and the disciples who never made the cut was that the plowman was ready. It's ultimately not about saying good-bye to your family or friends. It's not about giving a funeral or having a wedding. It's not about whether or not you go back to your town and throw a party and pass around meat to all the townspeople. It's about being ready for your moment when power unlocks potential.

Power released potential when Elijah tossed his mantle upon Elisha. The plowman got hit, and he could not go back to normal. Something inside Elisha changed. Even though he went back to kiss Mom and Dad good-bye, an allegiance had been broken inside him.

In Luke 9, the soul ties were still there. Those people were unwilling to follow Jesus and respond to His invitation because their hearts were knit to something, someone, or some life.

Elisha got hit with a mantle, and was messed up. He was ruined for the old ways and the old days. Even though the text tells us that he went back, his heart never went back. In fact, going back was Elisha's test. We'll look at this later, but God has different tests for different people. They are custom-made, for He evaluates us on an individual level.

I think that as Elisha prepared the farewell feast for his townsfolk, people were asking him, "Elisha, what are you doing? Where are you going? Why are you going off with that prophet? Why are you throwing your life away? Why don't you settle down? Get married. Have some kids. Get a good job. Work on your portfolio. Build up your retirement. Go on vacation. Carry on the family business."

Something kept Elisha's heart ready and receptive for transition. It was Elijah's response. After Elisha told his new mentor that he planned on going back home to say good-bye and throw a party, Elijah did not deem it a deal breaker. Elijah did not call him unfit for the new dimension he was being called into. It was obvious that Elisha was ready for his moment. All Elijah said was, *"Go on back, but think about what I have done to you"* (1 Kings 19:20b NLT). That's all Elijah *needed* to say.

When Elisha went home in the natural, his heart was still with Elijah. His allegiance was still with his invitation into his next season, new dimension, and greater glory. He was ruined and wrecked. I have to believe that during his trip back home, after crossing paths with Elijah, the former plowman was thinking:

I can't go back to being who I was. I can't act like it didn't happen. I can't ignore this whole new level of glory. I can't sit in that same place, even though loving hands pushed me there. I can't stay there, Mama. I love you, Daddy, it's been real. I know you had a plan for my future, and I hate to mess that up, but I've been exposed to power on another level. I've been unlocked and I've got to step into the next dimension.

One collision with power and you will never go back to normal again.

Get ready to step into your next dimension, into your next flame of glory, into your next supernatural release, into your next realm of the power of God. Like Elisha, you're being set up for an encounter with the glory of God. You're on track to getting all messed up. One collision with power and you will never be able to go back to normal again. There's no normal anymore. Normal has been redefined, upgraded, and supercharged. Your normal is now a whole new level!

Reflection Questions

1. In Luke 9:57-62, what prevented the three people from recognizing their moment and responding to Jesus?

2. What's on the other side of correctly responding to your moment?

3. How was Elisha's response to Elijah different from the examples in Luke 9?

CHAPTER 2

RESPOND TO YOUR MOMENT

Then he [Elisha] *arose and followed Elijah…*
(1 Kings 19:21).

RUINED FOR THE OLD LEVEL

*"Do not remember the former things,
nor consider the things of old. Behold, I
will do a new thing, now it shall spring
forth; shall you not know it? I will even
make a road in the wilderness and rivers
in the desert* (Isaiah 43:18-19).

Elisha had a meeting with power that redefined and reoriented his entire life. That's what power does to potential; it unlocks it! When potential is ready for its intersection with power, and the two collide, there is no going back. There is only one travel option—forward. Onward. Upward. The first thing we see is that Elisha *"arose and followed Elijah"* (1 Kings 19:21). It's time for you to arise and respond to your meeting with power.

In the previous chapter, we saw how Elisha's collision with power rendered him utterly useless in his old season. When your potential is called out by one moment with power, you become wrecked for living in your former season. You arise. You lift up your eyes. You see things on a new dimension. You see what you had not seen before. When you're ready for that new season and your moment comes, and power touches your life and releases what's inside you, there is no going back. You can try, but your plan will be foiled.

Someone may call and want you to come back, but the level of anointing that's been unlocked in your life cries out, "No, I won't settle for the old times, the old ways, the old fun, the old games, the old talk, the old hangouts. That satisfied me in my old season. That met some need inside of me while living in my former level. But you don't understand, I've been touched by power. Power was waiting all along.

"While we were having fun, the Maker of Heaven and earth was arranging a meeting. When we were hanging out, God Almighty was orchestrating a divine setup. He was getting ready to unlock my new glory. When we were on the golf course, in the nail salon, having a cheeseburger, something was happening in the unseen realm. You didn't see it, and I didn't know it, but something inside me was getting restless. Power was getting ready to come on the scene and show me who I am and unlock what's inside me. Now, I just can't go back!" Surely thoughts of this kind consumed

Elisha's mind as he walked through town and around the old neighborhood.

Elijah recognized that the touch of power would utterly ruin Elisha for everything that was back home in his old version of normal. We read that on Elisha's trip back to say good-bye to his old season, his old life, his old ways, his old routines, his old normals, his old friends, and his old job, he must have taken Elijah's instruction to heart.

When Elisha asked permission to go back home, Elijah did not scold or condemn him; he just left him with something to ponder. Elijah said, *"Go on back, but think about what I have done to you"* (1 Kings 19:20 NLT). I have to think that this one thought kept him ruined for the old while interacting with the old.

This is not some call to isolate yourself like a hermit. There are people and places that will not change, even when you are touched. Those collisions with power call out and unlock *your* potential; they do not release it for others. Each person must experience his or her own moment where power unlocks that person's potential. It's an intimate experience. Elijah's mantle was ready for Elisha—no one else. Even though there were 7,000 who had not bowed their knee to Baal and played the harlot before false gods, Elisha was the man who got the mantle.

As you come into contact with certain elements of your old level, don't belittle them. Don't shame them. Don't elevate yourself into some "above the rest" superiority position. God ordained you to make a transition from the old to the new for His purpose at this season according to His will. If others aren't there, just remember what took place in your life. If they try to invite you into their ways and activities, which were *your* old ways and old activities, smile and decline. You don't need to condemn others for not making the transition yet, just as others did not condemn you in your previous level.

God is patient with His people. He has a plan. Some just cooperate with it easier or more quickly than others. Rather than making anyone feel poorly about where they are, simply *live* at your new level. Speak at your new level. Operate at your new level. Don't flaunt it around. It's normal. It's natural. It's seamless. It feels right. It sounds good. This is just how you live now.

Normal for you is now the next level for somebody else. Live at your new normal, keeping in mind that your lifestyle is calling other people up higher. They see your potential released and something starts stirring within them. They see you operating in your gifts and talents, and they start wanting to steward what they have been given. Just encourage them to be faithful. That was the only thing that positioned you for the mantle transference.

Remember, Elisha faithfully plowed. He didn't run around looking for his moment. He didn't go to every service, conference, crusade, seminar, and motivational talk seeking out his moment. He was faithful in his old season and this positioned him to respond correctly at the most significant transition of his life. Most likely, Elisha had to deal with some of this thinking when he went back home to say good-bye to his old level. There was a whole town of people who were living in Elisha's old level.

Maybe there is a whole workplace of people living at your old level. Maybe you're in a house filled with people living at your old level. Maybe you are roommates with someone living on your old level. The best way you can summon them upward is by living at your new level as *normal*. It's no longer your next dimension—it's your normal dimension. It was the next level when you were living at the old level. It was an upgrade when you were out in the field plowing. But that was no longer the case for Elisha. The mantle was placed upon him. The next level quickly became his new level. The same is true for you!

HOW TO BE LAUNCHED
BY A MOMENT

The Lord was with Joseph, and he became a successful man, and he was in the house of his Egyptian master. His master saw that the Lord was with him and that the Lord caused all that he did to succeed in his hands. So Joseph found favor in his sight and attended him, and he made him overseer of his house and put him in charge of all that he had (Genesis 39:2-4 ESV).

Now I want us to look at what it means to live in this new dimension we have been launched into. There are people who get launched, but never learn how to live. They experience success, but they don't become *successful* like Joseph. They don't entertain a perspective where the touch of power transforms their entire mode of living. There are people who do experience a legitimate touch of power. It shakes them. It rattles them. It shifts stuff around. It heals. It delivers. It releases. It gives freedom. It makes them feel all good inside. Quickly, they were exposed to another dimension. The invitation was issued.

Now it's time to learn how to function at this new capacity. An experience is great, but it must be the gateway *into* something. It's one thing to stick your finger into an electrical socket and get shocked, but it's something else to learn how to live with a finger stuck in that socket. That's what I'm calling you to do. No, you're not always going to feel some zing, but you're going to know that what you felt, sensed, and experienced launched you into a new dimension of living. Going back is not an option. I just want you to have eyes that not only recognize your moment, but learn how to move forward *after* the moment.

Look at Elijah. All he did was pass Elisha by and let his mantle pass over the plowman. This was the moment when true power was exposed to true potential. Something happened in that moment that was undeniable and crystal clear. In fact, it was as if potential responded before power did. Power passed by potential, but potential dropped everything and ran after power. Again, potential recognized its moment; it was unlocked through an encounter with power. Potential quickly responded when power passed on by.

Read it again, *"Then Elijah passed by him and threw his mantle on him. And he left the oxen and ran after Elijah..."* (1 Kings 19:19-20). Elisha was ready for the next dimension. Not only did he recognize power's arrival, but he responded. He ran after it. You've got to want it that much.

Listen, God sovereignly sets you up, but you have to want it. You have to respond. You have to choose it. You have to run after it. When He brings you into a moment of power, don't fall down, spin around, jump on your head, and think to yourself, *Wow, that was a powerful touch!* The touch is never designed just to touch—the touch of power is designed to release you into the new level. Your moment is not about a moment, it's about a dramatic collision that will set the course of a whole new trajectory for your entire life.

Too many receive the touch, but don't follow the Teacher. Therein lies the test. Those who will not steward their moment are ultimately unable to step into a new season at that particular time of life. It doesn't mean God is done with them. It doesn't mean Jesus has passed them by. It just means there is more plowing to do. It just means that maturity, integrity, steadfastness, honor, and character need to be reinforced before people start living and functioning at a new dimension as a new normal.

You see, many are content to set up camp on the outskirts of a new dimension. They are fine fishing in the shallows when God's voice beckons them into the deep. They camp out on their moments of power, believing that the moment was all there was. Your moment was never designed to be sufficient—it was purposed to be a launching pad.

Consider how a diving board is not the final end, the pool is. People can jump up and down on a diving board all they want; it does not mean they are going to be launched from one level to the next, from land to water, from air to pool. Too many people live their lives jumping up and down on a spiritual diving board. Some moments may take them very high—they have dramatic encounters with power.

Just because you jump up does not mean you jump forward. Just because you go up does not mean you go forth. I've been assigned to call you up and send you forth.

This "up and down" thought process alone reveals that the person is not yet fit to go beyond the moment, jump forward, and step into the lifestyle. Imagine if Elisha had responded the way so many people today do to their moments of power.

If you can, try to reimagine the account in First Kings 19. Elisha could have responded to Elijah the way many believers respond to God's power today. He could have been plowing, caught the mantle, fallen down, rolled around, done some backflips, and then gone right back to plowing the same way he had always done it. He could have kept on plowing—his moment with Elijah just adding a spring to his step.

Let's never reduce our encounter with God's power to something that merely adds spring to our step. This is laughable. God does not bring Heaven's electricity to simply give you a thrill, but rather to give you a glimpse of what a new dimension of living looks like. The shock wakes you up to new levels of glory, anointing, power, realized potential, and activated purpose.

RESPOND TO YOUR MOMENT

The key is response. We must respond to our moment in order to live at another level. In order for potential to become released, we must respond to our moment of power.

In the previous chapter, we discovered how important it is to recognize your moment of power when it's standing before you. Elisha recognized Elijah and ran after him. Even after going back home and tying up some loose ends, Elisha still *arose* and followed him.

On the other side, the three people mentioned in Luke 9 did not truly realize the power of their moment, for they all responded poorly to their moment with Jesus. They encountered Him, but they did not follow Him. They had a moment, but the moment did not change or transform them. They were still clinging on to the comfort and safety of their former level of living. That's what they knew. That's what made sense. That's what they understood.

The new level of discipleship Jesus was extending their way was unsafe. It was radical. It was upside down. It was supernatural. They met Power as He walked down the road, but ultimately, they did not allow their moment with Power to launch them into a new dimension. That new dimension would have most likely meant their inclusion among the disciples in Luke 10 who were commissioned to transform the landscape of the known world. They were sent out as laborers, purposed to preach a new Kingdom and release the power of God. Truly, the seventy people in Luke 10 responded correctly to their moment of visitation, while the three nameless individuals in Luke 9 did not.

> **You have got to know when it's your moment—and do something about it.**

You have got to know when it's your moment—and do something about it. You've got to want it. Blind Bartimaeus knew when it was his moment, and even though they told him to shut up, shut up, shut up, he said, "I can't shut up! This is *my* moment!"

The man had an obvious impediment—his blindness. This could have been his excuse to bypass his moment. This could have been his out. This could have been his license to wallow in his old level and continue to be defined as *Blind Bartimaeus*. He decided to take another route. He used every faculty available to step into another level. Even though he could not see, he used what he had available—his hearing—to respond to his moment.

In Mark 10:47 we read how the story unfolds, *"And when he heard that it was Jesus of Nazareth, he began to cry out and say, 'Jesus, Son of David, have mercy on me!'"* He responded to his moment.

Even though Bartimaeus had an obvious physical handicap and although he experienced some significant resistance, he still used what he had to step into this moment. Why? He recognized what was on the other side of his collision with power. People told him to shut up, but he took that as fuel to cry out all the more and all the louder.

What are people telling you? Are they trying to keep you back from stepping into your new season? Are they wanting to restrain you from stepping into a new dimension, only to maintain you at their level? Press through. Recognize your moment and run after it like Elisha did. Silence the crowd by crying out louder like Bartimaeus did. Press through the crowd like the woman with the issue of blood (see Mark 5:25-34).

They saw their moments and responded. They were not content to let power pass by. They weren't after a fleeting touch or a mere thrill. They recognized that the touch of power was simply a transfer point that would launch them from one dimension to the next. From plowman to prophet. From blind man to disciple who could see (see Mark 10:52). From woman with a nonstop flow of blood to a daughter of God, healed and whole (see Mark 5:34). On the other side of each collision of power was a transformed life that still speaks to us today.

Reflection Questions

1. What does it mean to be "ruined for your old level"? What does this look like for you?

2. Is it possible to experience a touch of power but not see your life changed? What would this look like?

3. Can you identify examples of people who *correctly* responded to their moments of power and stepped into a new level?

CHAPTER 3

SEIZE YOUR MOMENT

...and [Elisha] *became his* [Elijah's] *servant* (1 Kings 19:21).

THE VALUE OF YOUR MOMENT

Elisha did not just receive a touch of power—he allowed that touch to transform and unlock his very identity. In First Kings 19:21, we see the result of Elisha's encounter with Elijah. He allowed the touch to transform him from plowman to Elijah's *servant*.

This is why your meeting with power is so vital and valuable. The key was *how* Elisha responded to the moment. He was not casual or cool about it. He was not lazy. He was not idle. Rather, he *seized* the moment and allowed it to transform him. We seize what we recognize as valuable and transformative.

> *You seize what you recognize as valuable and transformative.*

A moment of power is never given simply for the purpose of thrills and emotionalism. It is a transfer point. Don't be content to simply camp out on the outskirts of the possible when your moment has the power to call something out of you that *only* functions at a new, higher level. This is why stuff inside has not come to the surface yet. It's not that you don't have what it takes; you do. However, what's inside you is prepared and positioned for another level. If it came forth now, it would be destructive. If you started imparting and offering and sharing and releasing what you currently have stored up inside, no one would get it. You'd be written off. They'd say you're crazy. You've gone off the deep end.

I understand that with the release of potential, levels of persecution and resistance do come. However, there is also resistance that comes when we try to step out into our next season too early.

What's inside of you requires an intersection with power. The meeting is divine. It is sovereignly staged.

But remember, God does not set up these meetings just so you can get some type of spiritual high off the flowing current of His power. Your moment is intentional. It's designed to launch you into a new level where everything inside you will have its place to come forth.

Bartimaeus needed the divine intersection with the power of Jesus in order to become who he was created to be—a healed, seeing follower of the Lamb of God. He could not have made that happen in his own strength, nor could he have received any benefit from just seeking a touch without transformation. Every touch is designed for transformation.

In Mark 5, the woman with the constant flow of blood reached out and touched the hem of Jesus' garment. Power proceeded out of Him and ushered that woman into a transformative moment when her identity shifted. No longer was she the woman with the *"issue of blood"* (see Mark 5:25 KJV). Her moment changed her into one Jesus called *"Daughter,"* whose response to that moment *"made thee whole"* (see Mark 5:34 KJV).

Both these individuals pressed their way into transformation. They recognized the immeasurable value of a moment and seized it.. When a moment is good for nothing else but spiritual gymnastics, then we are content to simply receive a touch, when in fact God desires to release transformation. Bartimaeus would not have risked greater ridicule and cried out among the crowd if he did not expect a touch that transformed.

In the same way, the woman with the constant blood flow would not have left her home, crawled out into a very public place—where crowds were gathered around Jesus—and pushed herself through the masses to simply touch the edge of His robe if there was no expectation of transformation attached to this touch. She was not looking to feel good; she was looking to receive wholeness. She didn't want to live in her current level with some bells and whistles attached; she wanted to step into a whole new dimension of living. The value of the moment compelled these people to press through to Jesus.

Bartimaeus would not shut up. The woman didn't care if she had to crawl through the dirt in order to touch Power. This must be our attitude to seizing our new level. We can have no other approach to the transformative touch of power. I can't repeat it enough. A zing won't change you. Running around the building won't escort you to another level. You can touch the fire, feel the wind, and taste the rain, but if the extraordinary feelings that a touch of power brings are not accompanied by an extraordinary transformation, you're simply staying where you are with a good memory of how, one day, Elijah threw something on you and it made you feel good—but you didn't do anything with it.

You'll daydream about the exciting moment when Jesus came through town, and you didn't run, push, bite, crawl, wiggle, bicycle, or skateboard to get through the crowds and receive the touch that transformed everything. Why didn't you push through and receive from Him? You will never benefit from a moment of power if you do not recognize its value *beyond* a temporary feeling.

VISION PRODUCES RESOLVE AND TENACITY INSIDE YOU

Where there is no prophetic vision the people cast off restraint... (Proverbs 29:18 ESV).

Your moment is valuable because it has the ability to unlock your potential, and in turn, completely transform your identity. This is exactly what happened with Elisha. He responded correctly to his touch of power by following Elijah; and as a result of properly handling his moment, he went from plowman to prophet.

The same is true for you. When you have a vision for what your moment has the ability to produce in your life, you become tenacious. You have relentless resolve. You're not only going to get touched by a moment, but you are going to step into your moment.

People often experience a moment without ever stepping into the potential of that moment. That is what gets you from one level to the next. When you see this as the other side of your moment, you become like the people in the Gospel accounts who cast all inhibition aside because they knew their moment with Jesus would change everything. They seized it at all costs.

Is this you?

When your moment comes, don't just stand around. Start running. Your moment of power is an invitation into a lifestyle of unlocked potential and realized purpose. That's valuable! People spend all their lives chasing after these things. The wealthiest individuals on the planet would gladly surrender their entire fortunes for the very thing that presents itself to you in the form of a moment. Why? That moment unlocks the door to a greater release of your potential and greater fulfillment of your purpose.

Whatever it takes, go after it.

Whatever it takes, go after it. If you have to crawl, resolve to crawl into your moment. If you're knocked down on your knees, it doesn't matter. You're still coming in. This is tenacity. This is resolve. This is the grit that demonstrates whether or not you value what your moment has unlocked. Greater levels are not for the faint of heart. God protects people from greater levels because they don't see the value, and in turn, don't exhibit the vigor to walk upon those high places.

You may even see value in the collision before anyone else does. Think about the exchange between Elijah and Elisha. Elijah, the teacher, doesn't even realize the magnitude of what took place by exposing potential to power. He kept on walking. Was he ignorant? No. At the same time, he was waiting to see what would happen. Did Elisha, the student, value the touch? How was this plowman going to steward the mantle that was tossed upon him? Was he going to celebrate the touch and go back to plowing, or was the plowman going to receive the invitation to become a prophet.

Think about what happened between Jesus and the woman with the flow of blood. Many people were touching Him, but there was a touch that produced transformation. In fact, when the afflicted woman touched Jesus, Scripture tells us that *"power had gone out of Him"* (see

Mark 5:30). Jesus spun around and asked, *"Who touched My clothes?"* The disciples surely thought to themselves, *What is He hollering about?* They explained to Jesus, *"You see the multitude thronging You, and You say, 'Who touched Me?'"* (Mark 5:31). But there was something special about this woman's touch.

Scripture does not give us any additional clarity as to whether or not all of the other people who were thronging and touching Jesus were actually receiving from Him. Maybe they were, maybe not. Nevertheless, the text remains silent about these other people whose touch may or may not have produced transformative results. Vision is what caused this audacious woman to step into her moment. She had a vision for what touching Jesus would produce.

Even on her way to meet the Miracle Man, she was filled with vision and expectation. We read that *"She said, 'If only I may touch His clothes, I shall be made well'"* (Mark 5:28). In the *Amplified Bible* we are given a greater glimpse of how this woman responded to this vision. We read that *"She kept saying, 'If I only touch His garments, I shall be restored to health.'"* This was not some type of mantra. This was not a positive confession. This was not "put your mind to it, envision the outcome, and poof—it just happens out of the blue."

This woman was driven by a clear vision. She knew the touch of His power would unlock her potential. Her potential was wholeness. Her potential was receiving healing. Her potential was living without the incessant flow of blood that plagued her for twelve long, hard years. She had a vision for how the touch of power would unlock and release her potential so that, ultimately, she could fulfill her purpose. Power unlocks potential—and potential enables us to do what we have been designed to do.

This woman was restricted by her affliction. Her obstacle held her back from stepping into new levels of living, and ultimately, hindered her from fulfilling her purpose. Power destroys restrictions. It breaks through the chains that have held our potential back. The key is seizing our moments and responding to power when it shows up on the scene. When it walks in the door, something inside you will start leaping. What's happening? The potential inside you recognizes that the power that just walked in is the power that will draw it out.

DON'T LET YOUR TRANSITION PASS YOU BY

He who has a slack hand becomes poor, but the hand of the diligent makes rich (Proverbs 10:4).

Don't have a "slack hand" when it comes to seizing your moment. Proverbs 10:4 is a key for putting this principle into proper use. You have to grab it when it comes, and you have to hold on to it. If you don't seize it, you become poor. I'm not just talking about money. There are people with more money than they know what to do with, but they are still poor because they refuse to seize their moments.

Let's go back to Blind Bartimaeus. While the woman with the issue of blood took hold of her moment, Bartimaeus refused to let his moment pass him by. He knew that the power Jesus carried would unlock his potential and transition him to a new level. Jesus was passing through town, and this man responded. Let's look at the context and note the similarity between Bartimaeus and Elisha.

> *Now they came to Jericho. As He* [Jesus] *went out of Jericho with His disciples and a great multitude, blind Bartimaeus, the son of Timaeus, sat by the road begging. And when he heard that it was Jesus of Nazareth, he began to cry out and say, "Jesus, Son of David, have mercy on me!"* (Mark 10:46-47)

Just as Elisha could have missed Elijah, so Bartimaeus could have missed his moment with

Jesus. Bartimaeus responded to the fact that Jesus was coming through town. He started to cry out. People tried to shut him up, but this just was fuel for the fire. He upgraded his cry. He got louder. Maybe he got a bit wilder. He did whatever he could to get noticed—and he was. We see that *"Jesus stood still and commanded him to be called..."* (Mark 10:49). This was Bartimaeus' moment. And yet, it seemed like there was the possibility that he could have missed it—even now. Follow the rest of his story:

> *...Then they called the blind man, saying to him, "Be of good cheer. Rise, He is calling you." And throwing aside his garment, he rose and came to Jesus. So Jesus answered and said to him, "What do you want Me to do for you?..."* (Mark 10:49-51)

It was his turn. It was his time. It was his moment. In excitement, Bartimaeus got up, tossed aside his garment, and came over to Jesus. There they stood, face-to-face. Power locked eyes with blind potential. Jesus was getting ready to start fishing in this man's heart to see if he was ready for the transition. Even though Bartimaeus was blind, Jesus still asked, *"What do you want Me to do for you?"* Why such a question? It should have been obvious—right? The man was blind, and he wanted to see.

Think about it. Jesus was evaluating whether Blind Bartimaeus actually recognized the moment he was in, and if the man knew to what this moment would serve as a gateway. Jesus wanted to unlock potential, but He wanted to make sure that both He and Bartimaeus were on the same page. Jesus didn't want to just touch the guy; He wanted to heal him. Jesus didn't want to pat him on the back and comfort him in the affliction. His heart of compassion moved Him toward healing, so that the healing could offer a whole new way of living for the blind man.

There is a chance that the blind man could have responded incorrectly to Jesus' question.

He could have given an answer that unveiled a heart not capable of carrying a new dimension of glory. He could have simply asked Jesus for a touch—and no more. He could have thrown a pity party, elevating the status of his affliction above the power that Jesus had available to release and unlock Bartimaeus' potential. I know this sounds ridiculous considering who was standing before the blind man, but this example speaks volumes to believers today.

So many of us stand before power and give the wrong answer. We give wrong answers because of how demanding, how outlandish, how supernatural, and how impossible the right ones sound. We give wrong answers because we want to be safe rather than seize the moment in front of us. But if you don't seize it, it will pass you by. I don't care how wild it sounds.

If you heard that Jesus had the power to heal blind people and you were Blind Bartimaeus, you would seize that opportunity no matter how ridiculous the prospect of a miracle sounded. If you had to stand on your head and turn cartwheels, it wouldn't matter. Power is standing before you, and that power is the only catalyst that will release your potential.

The key is, you have to want it, and that intense desire has to exceed your mind's tendency to rationalize. Jesus was familiar with the natural mind. He knew that Bartimaeus might have been in a wrestling match with logic and reason and common sense. "Miracles don't happen." "That's impossible!" "Blind people don't see—they are blind!" We don't know what transpired in his mind. All we know is that he heard Jesus had come into town, and he seized his moment. He knew that regardless how impossible it sounded, Jesus was the only One who could release his potential.

Bartimaeus gave Jesus the correct answer. In responding to Jesus's question, he said, *"Rabbi, I want to see"* (see Mark 10:51 NLT). The result? *"Instantly the man could see, and he followed Jesus down the road"* (Mark 10:52 NLT). It was more than a touch. It was more than a healing. It was more than a miracle or a moment.

Bartimaeus was launched into his purpose because he seized his moment, experienced the touch of power, saw potential unlocked, and was propelled into purpose. His ultimate purpose? Although healing was part of his purpose, the end result of his healing was that Bartimaeus could now become one who *followed Jesus*.

Reflection Questions

1. How should you appropriately respond to the divine moments that God brings into your life? How did Elisha respond?

2. What does it mean to recognize the value of your moment? How will a vision of its value change the way you respond to it?

3. What stands out to you from the example of Blind Bartimaeus—how he responded to his power meeting with Jesus?

CHAPTER 4

NO RETURN TO THE ORDINARY

And he left the oxen and ran after Elijah, and said, "Please let me kiss my father and my mother, and then I will follow you." And he [Elijah] said to him, "Go back again, for what have I done to you?" (1 Kings 19:20).

GET MESSED UP FOR THE USUAL

I now want us to look at *what is produced* when power meets potential. Even though it's a brief moment in time, it is a moment that is absolutely pregnant with purpose. Remember, it's the divine intersection of power and potential that brings us into purpose. Your meeting with power is your God-extended invitation into a life that is messed up for everything it used to be.

The divine intersection of power and potential brings you into purpose.

Let's rewind a little bit and go back to when Elijah tossed his mantle onto Elisha. The plowman knew what had taken place. It didn't demand a discussion. He knew that the mantle Elijah threw upon him demanded *everything*. This is why he told Elijah that he wanted to go back home to kiss his father and mother goodbye. The same was true with Blind Bartimaeus. The truth is, he was blind one minute; but because of his moment with power, he could now see—blindness is a highly unsatisfying reality to consider returning to.

Likewise, when you have been bleeding for twelve years, and then because of the power you experienced in a single moment the bleeding stops, the mere notion of going back to the bleeding is repulsive. There is nothing back there. Nothing in the plowing. Nothing in the blindness. Nothing in the bleeding.

Each of these people experienced a different set of circumstances, but each had a single common denominator—they were invited into a new level. Each one had a collision with power that brought them into a new dimension. Each individual experienced a most unique promotion.

Your promotion makes the plow work of yesterday highly unsatisfying. The very thing that positioned you for promotion can actually rob you of the blessing of promotion if, like Lot's wife, you look back. Jesus tells us to *"Remember Lot's wife"* (Luke 17:32). What's so important about this lady and her decision to look back? As Lot and his family were fleeing the city of Sodom and Gomorrah, which the Lord had marked for destruction, they were given a very clear set of instructions: *"Do not look behind you nor stay anywhere in the plain. Escape to the mountains, lest you be destroyed"* (Genesis 19:17). Why? There was nothing back there for them to look at. It was a city in ruins.

Lot and his family had an intersection with power. God paid them a visit in the form of two rescuing angels (see Genesis 19:1). Power was delivering these people out of a dying city. Power pulled them out of that dark place where who they truly were would never be recognized or realized. There was potential inside Lot and his family that remained untapped as long as they remained in the depravity of Sodom.

The problem was, something inside Lot's wife was still connected to the old life, the old ways, the old friends, the old places. Something inside her was still deeply attached to how things used to be—so much so that she directly disobeyed the angelic instructions they received. When she looked back, she turned into the very thing that the city became, a *"pillar of salt"* (see Genesis 19:26).

> **God is calling you out of what you have known and is inviting you into the deep waters.**

Maybe Lot's wife thought she could enjoy the best of both worlds. God was calling Lot and his family into the high places. He was calling them up, into the mountains (see Genesis 19:17). Lot's wife was trying to save something that was infinitely inferior to what she was being invited into.

In some way, Lot's wife was in bondage to her old life. The prospect of stepping into something new might have been overwhelming. Maybe she was terrified. She had known Sodom. This was her stomping ground. She knew the streets. She knew the city. Maybe she was friends with the neighbors. She knew that Mr. Jones came out every morning at 8:30 and watered the plants. She knew that Mrs. Jenkins walked the dog after dinner at 6 o'clock. She had a schedule. She had a system. She had a routine.

Do you see where I'm going with this? God is calling you out of what you have known and is inviting you into the deep waters. You are being beckoned to abandon the familiar and the comfortable and the safe, and step out into an entirely new dimension of living.

Sadly, many never actually take this step because the stability of the familiar and comfortable restrain them.

THE EXTRAORDINARY IS CALLING

> *So Abram went, as the Lord had told him, and Lot went with him. Abram was seventy-five years old when he departed from Haran. And Abram took Sarai his wife, and Lot his brother's son, and all their possessions that they had gathered, and the people that they had acquired in Haran, and they set out to go to the land of Canaan...* (Genesis 12:4-5 ESV).

Sometimes the comfort of an old season tries to keep us from embracing the new thing God wants to launch us into. We prefer the ordinary, because the extraordinary has too much uncertainty attached to it. The ordinary is what we are being invited out of. The ordinary was all fine and good for its season, but now the God of the Extraordinary is calling. Your name is up!

Let's not be like Lot's wife who ultimately rejected the summons to step out of her old season. She responded just the opposite of Lot's uncle, Abraham. When his moment came, *Abram went, as the Lord had told him* (see Genesis 12:4 ESV). He moved toward the unknown and unfamiliar. This was his pathway to promotion.

It's amazing how even if the place where we are living is destructive, like Sodom, or idolatrous like Haran, we still stay because it's familiar. Abram did not, but Lot did. Why? There's comfort in what has become our ordinary. Even if we're blind, even if we're bleeding, some are content to stay in the comfort of their pain instead of stepping forward into the unknown of their purpose. Purpose is only unknown because we have not stepped *in* yet. When power calls us, we must respond, for it's in our response where potential is realized and unlocked.

> *Some are content to stay in painful comfort rather than stepping into perfect purpose.*

For some of us, our pain and problems became a source of perverted comfort because they gave us something to fall back on as we were being summoned out into the unknown. Hear me out, I'm not saying that pain, in and of itself, is comfortable. It's not. It stings. It hurts. It restrains. It withholds. It debilitates. It harms. It hinders. Pain is not comfortable; but for some people, they have chosen to identify themselves with their pain.

Blind Bartimaeus was recognized as "Blind Bartimaeus." Maybe people identified him by his condition like a nickname. Perhaps this is why Jesus was asking him, "What do you want Me to do for you?" when it seemed like his need was quite obvious! But as I mentioned earlier, I think Jesus was searching for something. He wanted to see if this man was really serious, not just about receiving a touch, but about getting a name change. Jesus wanted to see how deeply blindness was ingrained in Bartimaeus' identity.

In the same way, Elisha was faced with a choice. His situation was different, although the principle is the same. Even though he was not caught in a debilitating situation, he was nevertheless living at a former level. He was plowing when the invitation to purpose passed him by. Was Elisha going to remain "Elisha the plowman," or would he step into the role of "Elishathe prophet"?

Consider the ramifications for just a moment. If Elisha did not respond to the mantle of

Elijah and just kept on plowing because plowing is what he knew and plowing was his safety net and plowing was familiar, the prophetic calling assigned to his life would never have been realized.

On the other side of each power-filled moment is a release of unlocked potential that completely changes every life.

On the other side of each power-filled moment is a release of unlocked potential that completely changes every life. Blind Bartimaeus got healed and became a Christ-follower. Elisha became a prophet who walked in a double portion of the anointing that was upon Elijah. Consider the result of Elisha saying "Yes" to the unknown and unfamiliar.

Elisha stepped into a realm of miracles that even Elijah had not experienced. These miracles, and the lives they impacted, would have never been realized or demonstrated if Elisha had kept on plowing. If he stayed behind in his old realm, in his former glory, in his previous position, he would not have been privileged to participate in the extraordinary exploits that were only activated when he stepped out. If he had decided to keep plowing, his eyes would not have seen the Jordan River divided (see 2 Kings 2:14). If he had chosen to remain a plowman and forfeit his opportunity to become a prophet, he would not have performed a creative miracle that healed the waters at the spring of Jericho (see 2 Kings 2:21).

Understand, all of this potential was available to Elisha. *This* is exactly what was unlocked at the moment of the divine meeting, when Elijah's power unlocked Elisha's potential. Maybe his eyes didn't see it all right there when he caught Elijah's mantle. And in your moment of power, you probably won't see the entire plan. Every detail, every stop along the road, every blessing, every meeting, every breakthrough— your mind would not be able to handle it all right there in a single encounter with power. You don't need to know. All you need to understand is that the moment of power activates potential to do things your imagination cannot even conceive.

Second Kings tells us that Elisha went on to miraculously provide oil for the widow woman (4:1-4), raised her son from the dead (4:35), purified food (4:41), multiplied bread (4:43), healed Naaman's leprosy (5:10), caused a metal ax head to float (6:6), and saw blindness healed (6:17).Even a dead man was raised to life because his lifeless body came into contact with the anointed bones of Elisha (13:21). Even after Elisha was dead, buried, and decayed to the point where only his bones were left, the power upon that prophet's physical frame was so strong, so potent, that just by coming into contact with it, healing broke out. *This* is what that one moment of power released Elisha to do, both in his life and after he had died.

I wonder what God is getting ready to release inside you!

Yes, in the stepping-out process there is mystery. One moment Elisha was plowing and the next he felt a mantle hit his shoulders. There was mystery in what all of this entailed. Elisha didn't have all the answers. He didn't get some instant download of the complete course of action that would follow his collision with power. He just knew something was shifting. He was ready, he was willing, and in turn he responded.

Don't dare settle for the comfort of some old, worn-out season when you are being beckoned and brought into the unknown. It's only unknown because you haven't experienced it yet. You haven't touched it. You haven't tasted it. You haven't smelled it. You haven't seen it. It's unknown because it's not the familiar. It's not the ordinary. It's not what you've always known. It's not where you've been. It's something fresh, something new, and something that's going to shake everything.

> *Don't settle for worn-out known when you can step into His glorious unknown.*

CHANGE YOUR IDENTITY

The problem for some of us is that the old season, even though it was destructive, is something that we are familiar with, and by continuing to live in that old season of familiar pain, we prevent ourselves from stepping out into the new season of unfamiliar purpose. Somewhere along the line, we identified self with a season.

Good or bad, we cannot identify ourselves by a season, for when the season changes, we get worried. We start shaking. We're nervous. Why? Because who we aree is changing. Instead we need to celebrate. If you were Blind Bartimaeus in your former season, I've got good news. You're about to become Healed

Bartimaeus. You're about to become Blessed Bartimaeus. You're about to become Bartimaeus, the disciple. Don't ever hold on to some identity you embraced in your former season, because it might have been wrong.

You need to know who you are, absolutely. You need to know who you are and what you have in Christ. You need to know your strengths and weaknesses. You need to be familiar with your faults and foibles. You need to know what you're good at, what you're wired for, and how you've been programmed. Those are healthy identities that carry you through any and every season.

There are unhealthy identities like Blind Bartimaeus, when you become identified by your plight or problem. When your addiction labels you. When your bondage becomes a badge. When your name is determined by your enemy.

Embrace the shift. When power unlocks your potential, God wants to break that false identity and build a correct one.

Beyond unhealthy identities, there are simply old-season identities you need to deal with. I've said it before, God has called you to be faithful where you are, doing what you're doing—*for now.*

Elisha was a plowman, and he faithfully fulfilled this assignment and identity. However, when power unlocked his potential, his profession shifted. His identity changed. What was right yesterday would be wrong today if he tried to continue in that same identity. If Elisha sought to remain *the plowman* while trying to step into his identity as *the prophet,* he would be stepping right into a nervous breakdown. The plowman made it possible for the prophet to emerge. Remember, Elisha was faithful as the plowman and then he was elevated.

Promotion was the by-product of faithfulness in the previous season. But when the moment comes and the mantle hits, you have to think on your feet. Don't hang on to a past identity when God is bringing you into a new present reality.

There are elements of the plowman that will carry over into the prophet. The ability to plow and press and work and toil to break up ground—the very character that the plowman developed in Elisha positioned him to step into his new identity of prophet. These characteristics would continue. They would make the cut. They would endure the transition.

Just like who you are—your strengths, your abilities, your knowledge, your skill sets, your wisdom, and your aptitudes. Everything that will keep you moving forward will endure the mantle. Everything from yesterday that will help you step further into today will continue into the new dimension.

At the same time, the stuff that holds you back cannot endure. It cannot go on through. It just can't, as it has no place. You can't let it. Your moment with power exposes you to what can continue—and what cannot. Your glimpse of the next dimension gives you vision for what you can take with you and what you can't take. The only things you can't take are the things that will sabotage your forward momentum.

Just know things aren't going to be like they used to be. Old things might be calling your name, trying to get you to look back. You can't go there. They'll try to convince you that comfortable is better. You just remind them what's on the other side of your unknown and unfamiliar.

Elisha stepped into the unknown and unfamiliar and he lived at a new dimension. He walked in a greater anointing. He experienced greater glory. The miracles were greater. He pressed into realms that Elijah never knew.

God has said, *"Behold, the former things have come to pass, and new things I declare; before they spring forth I tell you of them"* (Isaiah 42:9). After your meeting with power, you may go back to the same address, but you will not be the same person, because God has done a fresh thing in your life. I repeat, you cannot go back.

After meeting with power, you will not be the same person–God has done a fresh thing in you.

You might try. Elisha did. He tried to go back to his old normal after the meeting, and nothing fit. Nothing made sense. Nothing came close to what he had just received when power passed by. You will go back and look at what you used to call good and say, "What in the world was I thinking?" Whenever God elevates you to the next level, you look at things that you used to call excellent and ask, "What happened to them?" They didn't change. You changed. You received an upgrade. You received a mantle. You were a plower, but now you are a prophet. There's nothing wrong with the ox. There's something right with you—you've been exposed to the next level of glory, and it's time for you to step on in.

Reflection Questions

1. Why is it intimidating to leave the ordinary and familiar behind?

2. How is it possible for people to use pain as a source of comfort? Why does this prevent you from stepping into the next season?

3. What are the benefits of stepping out into the unknown and unfamiliar?

CHAPTER 5

MAKE FIREWOOD

So Elisha turned back from him, and took a yoke of oxen and slaughtered them and boiled their flesh, using the oxen's equipment, and gave it to the people, and they ate... (1 Kings 19:21).

MAKE FIREWOOD OUT OF THE OLD POSITION

When potential has awakened it will never rest again. *It will never rest again.* Potential did not orchestrate the meeting; it just happened, but since it happened, potential says:

- "I know this is what I've been waiting for all of my life."

- "This is my moment, and I cannot ignore the power to which I have been exposed."

- "I have been plowing on the twelfth yoke of oxen. I cannot go back and assume the family business."

Elisha went back to his home, but did not go back to life on the old level. Even though he physically stood among his family and friends and former living conditions, he was now functioning at the next level.

You can still live in the next dimension among those who are still in a former level. You are responsible for *you*. You are the one who received the mantle. Trust God's timing and divine orchestration to deal with others who are not living at the next level. You're not God's commissioned constable. You're not His holy law enforcement agent. Your goal is not to make people feel badly about their present level when you are living in the next. No—you run with what you have. You live at that next level, and the onlooking world will want what you have.

When Elisha went home, he made a decision. Look at what he does:

> *So Elisha returned to his oxen and slaughtered them. He used the wood from the plow to build a fire to roast their flesh...* (1 Kings 19:21 NLT).

The man was serious about moving forward. In this moment, the shift is established. He received the mantle, but he could have gone back home...and stayed. He could have decided that the future was too frightening and succumbed to playing it safe as a plowman, living with Momma and Daddy. The opportunity was obviously there. But Elisha was cut from a different cloth. The man was made of more than that. He was not intimidated by what was before him. He made a decision in his heart that next level living was his only option; and as a result, he took what represented his former life and identity—the oxen and the plow—and broke it up and made firewood out of it.

God will make firewood out of your former position!

God is going to make firewood out of your former position! There are things you might be laying down, but there are characteristics and qualities you are upgrading. There's stuff that's changing its very structure and makeup as you embrace transition. Elisha's plow—which fueled the fire—represented Elisha's past. He was a plowman, and that plow became the fire that destroyed any option of going back to yesterday. Instead, it became a fire that fueled his forward trajectory into a new tomorrow. Elisha's past was his profession. Even though the ox became dinner and the plow became firewood, the things that Elisha gleaned through being a plowman were set ablaze in the fire of surrender.

In the same way that Moses threw down his shepherd's rod before the Lord and it was empowered to accomplish the supernatural (see Exodus 4:1-4), so Elisha throws down what he has—the ox and the plow—and it becomes the fire that launches him into the next glory.

FUEL FOR THE NEXT GLORY

God doesn't want to destroy you; He wants to elevate you. A rod in Moses' hand could only accomplish natural things. He could lead sheep. That was Moses' ordinary. That was what he had known and that was his realm of familiarity. God was not looking to take away his shepherd's staff; He was looking to touch it with power and unlock potential. Let's look at Moses' story, for it illustrates what's going on with Elisha.

> *So the Lord said to him, "What is that in your hand?" He said, "A rod." And He said, "Cast it on the ground." So he*

cast it on the ground, and it became a serpent... (Exodus 4:2-3).

The same God is asking you, "What is that in your hand?" Are you still clinging to the plow of yesterday while trying to live in a new dimension? God doesn't want to snatch your plow away. He doesn't want to steal your shepherd's rod. He's not on some quest to make your life miserable and take all of your stuff away. No, He wants to make the devil miserable by getting you to hand your stuff over to Him, and let Him infuse it with power. He wants to ignite what you have. The key is yielding it to Him. If He sets the plow on fire while you're holding it, it's going to hurt. It's going to burn. If you don't let go, and the fire consumes it, you will die. You won't be able to sustain the fire. It will kill you, not promote you.

God doesn't set plows on fire while they are still in the care of the plowman; in the same way, He doesn't turn rods into serpents while they are still being held by the shepherd. Why? Because if we are unwilling to submit these things to God, we are unable to sustain what He wants to release through them.

God wants to take the very things that define your position and profession and set them on fire.

God wants to take the very things that define your position and profession and set them on fire. That's living in a new dimension. It can be shocking because it's so different. Moses was shocked when his shepherd's rod turned into a serpent. In Exodus 4:3, Moses watches the supernatural transformation of staff to snake, and we read that *"Moses fled from it."* We cannot be intimidated by the next level of glory.

God's taking things we were comfortable with and charging them with supernatural power. Skills we had in the old season are being touched by His power. Potential's coming out that we didn't know was there. It shocks us. We're frightened. At times, we want to run away. The whole thing is too glorious, and a bit too much.

But you can't go back.

The plow's burning. The ox is dead and cooked. People are eating its flesh. You've gone too far and there is no reversing it. Keep going. The same staff that scared Moses saved the nation of Israel. The rod that led sheep was the same rod that led God's chosen people out of bondage. God's taking your old position and setting it on fire. Moses led sheep in the wilderness in one level; but in the next, he led people in the wilderness. Elisha plowed the ground in one dimension; but in the next, he plowed the soil of human hearts to receive the seed of God's prophetic word.

I dare you to get excited about God taking what you had in your previous level and anointing it in a new level.

MAKE FIREWOOD OUT
OF YOUR PAST

Elisha's plow was not only his position and profession, it also symbolized his past. This is what he had known and had been defined by. He was Elisha the plowman. We've already talked about the need to leave the past behind, move forward, and refuse to look back. I want to take it a step further. I want to take this opportunity to encourage you that the same God who sets fire to your profession and position can also set fire to your past.

It's one thing to talk about how God uses our talents and our giftings and our accolades and our triumphs—it's another thing to talk about how He uses our past. And I'm not talking about your past as a schoolteacher, your past as a dentist, your past as a construction worker, your past as a taxi driver, your past as the star quarterback for the high school football team. It's easy to accept that He uses these things because they are safe.

> *The same God who sets fire to your profession and position can also set fire to your past.*

I don't want to play it safe and keep it cute. I don't want to talk about the good stuff; I want us to get into the grit. It's one thing to believe God uses your past successes—it's another level of thinking that emboldens us to believe that He wants to use our past failures, messes, mistakes, shortcomings, train wrecks, disgraces, shame, and sins.

When power hits potential, we run—we don't argue. We don't argue with power, giving it every reason why we shouldn't be called. We give God our reasons, "But God, don't You know who I am? Don't You know what I've done?" Power comes; and instead of embracing it, we resist it. We remind power that our past disqualifies us for the present calling. We try to persuade power that we are unworthy of the summons because in our past we may have squandered our potential.

Let me remind you, God is not a man and does not operate according to how we think He should work. Your past does not intimidate Him. We remind God of our past as if He is clueless about what happened. When He summons us, it is absolutely ridiculous to start reminding Him why He should *not* be calling us. He knows what He's doing. He's not blind. He's seen our faults. He sees our struggles. Those things done in the darkness that no one else knows about. God saw them, and He still loves you. Those memories that bring you shame every time you invite them back into your mind.

God was there. He was there in the darkness, and He was there in the light. He was there when you were with the person you shouldn't have been with, and He was there when you weren't in the place you should have been. He was there in the pit, and He was there in the palace. He was there when you lied. He was there when you cheated. He was there when you smudged your taxes. He was there when you lost your mind. He was there when you crossed the line. He saw every moment, still loves you, and is still summoning you. Don't insult Him by asking, "Why me?"

None of us deserve anything. We didn't go looking for grace; grace came banging down our door. We're not good enough for God. Nothing inside of us cried out for God to come and rescue us; He put that cry inside of us. That's all true. Paul says it best:

> *And you were dead in the trespasses and sins in which you once walked, following the course of this world, following the prince of the power of the air, the spirit that is now at work in the sons of disobedience—among whom we all once lived in the passions of our flesh, carrying out the desires of the body and the mind, and were by nature children of*

wrath, like the rest of mankind (Ephesians 2:1-3 ESV).

This is our past. If anyone had a problem past, it was the apostle Paul. He persecuted and killed Christ followers. He was a murderer. He was the worst of the worst. He recognized this, writing of himself, *"I am the least of the apostles, who am not worthy to be called an apostle, because I persecuted the church of God"* (1 Corinthians 15:9).

Paul had a past. Maybe you had a past. Does this exclude you from the present purpose of God? No. Even after Paul gives us the list in Ephesians 2, reminding us of every bad, wretched, and unspeakable thing we had done, we are invited into a new present and a new future. God is not blind to our former trespasses. He watched as we walked in league with the devil, doing his bidding. He saw as we made passions and lusts our gods and idols.

We think the next verse should be a disqualifier, when in fact it simply reads, *"But God..."*

(Ephesians 2:4). These two words are your invitation to live in a new reality where your past is not counted against you.

Paul continues:

> *But God, being rich in mercy, because of the great love with which He loved us, even when we were dead in our trespasses, made us alive together with Christ—by grace you have been saved—and raised us up with Him and seated us with Him in the heavenly places in Christ Jesus"* (Ephesians 2:4-6 ESV).

Power brought you into a whole new dimension of living. Your present and your future are not dictated by your past. In fact, God uses your past as a tool of measurement. Your past reminds you how far He's brought you and how deep you've gone. This is how power makes firewood out of the past.

When you view your past in light of your present summons, your heart is ignited. You can't shut down the thanksgiving. You know you're not worthy, but He called you worthy. Of course you're not deserving, but God said you are deserving. The King is calling. The courier is handing off the royal invitation. Don't hide your face. Don't run off into the shadows in shame. Stand tall. Remember where you came from, but feel the fire of where He's bringing you.

Your present and your future are not dictated by your past.

If you don't have a past, you don't have the fire. I believe God wants to take your past and make firewood out of it. It will be the flame that ignites your future, sets off your destiny, creates your passion for your purpose, and releases you into another dimension. The past brings everything into perspective.

Set the ox on fire. Turn that ox into food and feed the neighborhood. Elisha might have said, "This can feed you, but it can't feed me. I cannot continue to follow a dumb thing. I know I've got some more rows to be plowed, but I cannot stay in my position, for the traditions of men will make the Word of God of no effect. If I continue to stay in the sensible circle, making the acceptable motions, trying to live up to the status quo, I am going to miss my moment. So here, you eat it. It's not that it is bad. It was good for me at one time—but a shift has occurred."

Reflection Questions

1. How can you make firewood out of your position or profession? How does it provide fuel for your next level?

2. What does it mean to make firewood out of your past?

3. How should you respond to your past when God summons you into your future?

CHAPTER 6

LIVE ON A NEW LEVEL

...Then he [Elisha] arose and followed Elijah, and became his servant (1 Kings 19:21).

DISCOVER WHO YOU BECAME

No longer shall your name be called Abram, but your name shall be Abraham; for I have made you a father of many nations (Genesis 17:5).

In the same way that Abram received a divine name change to Abraham, Elisha experienced a similar transformation. Elisha returned from burning the plow and feeding the ox to the townsmen, and stepped right into the flow of his next level. We read that Elisha *"arose and followed Elijah, and became his servant"* (1 Kings 19:21). Note the word *became*.

Elisha was not dating a new dimension. He wasn't flirting with it. He wasn't testing out the waters. He wasn't satisfied with a touch of power that made him feel good, but didn't transform his life. The result of Elisha's meeting with Elijah? Power awakened potential, and potential was unlocked. Elisha stepped into his new identity. He *became* Elijah's servant.

He didn't walk with Elijah for a little while, get tired, and then go back to plow and cook oxen with the folks back home. Home was redefined for Elisha. "Plan B" was removed from his equation. His only option was moving forward with Elijah, because when you become something, it's difficult to unbecome it.

When you *do* something, you can stop doing it. Elisha could have *done* the whole serving thing for Elijah, but then turned back when things stopped making sense. When Elijah got too cranky, Elisha could have said, "This is not for me. I don't want to deal with you and your temper and your craziness and your strangeness. I'm out, I'm through. I served for a season, but now I'm going back." There's no going back for someone who *became* something.

> **There's no going back for someone who became something.**

When the teacher was taken up in the flaming chariots, Elisha could have turned back and run for his life. "I didn't sign up for this. I wasn't planning on this taking place. Nobody warned me. Nobody told me what was coming. I want out."

If Elisha chose to simply serve Elijah as an act, it would have been easier for him to turn back. But Elisha's encounter with power didn't just sustain him for a season. His DNA was changed. The plowman started to become a prophet when he *became* Elijah's servant.

THE LOW PERSON IN A NEW LEVEL

> *And whoever exalts himself will be humbled, and he who humbles himself will be exalted* (Matthew 23:12).

Somebody might say, "Well, Elisha, you're still following." He says, "Yeah, but I'm following on a whole different level." He wasn't following an ox, he was following a prophet. What he was following before was the family business. He was following the trajectory of his history. Now he was following in the direction of his destiny.

The same is true for you. Don't get discouraged if the encounter with power has you still following something or someone. Following is not the problem; it's what or who you're following that determines at what level you choose to live. Was Elisha going to keep following around an animal, or was he going to follow Elijah?

> **I'd rather be the low man in my destiny**
> **than the lead man in my history.**

Elisha did not mind following. Why? When you're following at a new level, everything's different. I'd rather be the low man in my destiny than the lead man in my history. You know what I'm talking about. That moment comes when we're invited into a new level, and what happens? We look back at what *was*, because what *was* kept us in a high position. But where was that high position? Elisha's "high position" was following around an ox and plowing. Elisha's position might have been high in his old season; but now, he was invited into a whole new dimension of living. He was exposed to a realm of reality beyond his current living conditions. Yes, he was going to have to start at the bottom, following Elijah, but I'd rather follow Elijah into my purpose any day than stay around in some worn-out season that holds nothing else for me.

The same is true for you.

Don't get discouraged if you keep following into your new season. Think about it. You're not following an ox anymore, you're following Elijah. You're following the person or the thing or the opportunity or the business or the career or the idea or the path that is taking you into the next level. You see, the season of the ox prepared Elisha for living at the next level, but it would never bring him into the next level.

Where you were, before your meeting with power, had its purpose—in its season. Your old season made sense *before* power came walking by. But it makes no sense for us to choose to remain in the old season. I don't care if you're the prince in your old season when power pays a visit, because the pauper in the new season is leagues ahead of the prince in an old season.

Now, you're going to come in on the bottom level of a new dimension. Up until this point, everybody in your life has been pulling after you, looking to you for answers, looking for solutions, calling you about this, and calling you about that because you were the plower of the twelfth yoke of oxen. That was your identity in the old season. You were large and in charge. You felt special. You had the answers. You knew the solutions. You got it all figured out.

But don't be afraid. In the new season, you're going to start out knowing nothing, and I'd rather know nothing in the new than keep on knowing everything in the old. You're carrying what you learned in the old season into the new season. God's not erasing your memory. The key is, you're stepping into the unfamiliar and unknown. Celebrate it. Every step you take toward where you don't have a clue where you're going, be confident that you are walking farther toward your purpose. Your potential is being released. You're taking significant strides toward fulfilling destiny.

HOW TO WALK IN THE DARK

For we walk by faith, not by sight
(2 Corinthians 5:7).

We throw around phrases like, "Walk by faith, not by sight." In church, when the preacher talks about this truth, we shout "Amen" and get excited; but when everything changes and we start walking in the dark, we cannot depend on sight. What you've seen has not prepared you for where you're going. What you saw in the old season won't help you as you begin navigating your new dimension.

If Elisha tried to see life from a plowman's perspective in his new season, he would have been lost. He didn't know from what perspective he would be seeing. The terrain was alien. All he knew was this guy passed by him, tossed his mantle upon his shoulders, and kept on going. Using what sense he had, Elisha had to assume that this prophet who passed by and kept on walking *knew* where he was going.

Elisha didn't know where Elijah was going, but Elijah looked like he knew. In turn, Elisha followed the leader.

Faith is your anchor and sustainer in the new season. Faith that the One who called us is faithful (see 1 Thessalonians 5:24). Faith that our steps are ordered by the Lord (see Psalm 37:23). Faith helps you see in the dark. And when you feel like you can't see, faith steadies your heart to trust what you know. What is true. What is constant. What is unchanging. What is invisible. Faith is the only way you are able to see in the dark of transition.

> *Faith is the only way we are able to see in the dark of transition.*

Earlier on, we studied how your meeting with power transitions you into a realm of unfamiliarity and unknowability. You don't know where you're going because it's unfamiliar. It's unfamiliar because you've never been there.

Now, I want to help you learn how to walk in the dark. That's what living at a new level is like. You're walking forward. You may not see where you're going, but you know that you're walking. You put one foot in front of the other. Things aren't clear. They don't make sense. You may trip and fall. There's even a good chance you're going to fail and make a mistake. That's okay. It's legal.

I'd choose failure in a new dimension over success in an old season that's passed me by. Think about it. Success in an old season actually does not move you forward into your destiny and purpose. If you choose to stay behind in the old and settle for success as a plower, when you're really called to be a prophet, you could be the most successful plower there is, but your purpose as a prophet is still waiting for you to step up.

You're going into a new dimension, living at a new level. With it comes a level of uncertainty, a level of humility, a level where you have to learn and you have to grow and you have to pray and you have to read. This will be unfamiliar territory. For all of your life, up until now, you have been operating in the familiarity of your comfort zone. You do the same things over and over again, following the routine that you always knew. You had the field mapped out and knew every corner and every crevice. You understood it. You knew where the rocks were. You knew where the roots were. You knew where the snakes hid. You knew where the opposition was. You knew where everything was.

Your life was defined by the old system and old cycle. But ever since power hit, your potential is coming out and it demands something new. The old wineskin can't contain what's about to break forth in your life.

BREAK THE CYCLE

...but one thing I do, forgetting those things which are behind and reaching forward to those things which are ahead (Philippians 3:13).

I want you to proactively pursue discomfort. You read this right—don't adjust your eyes. This is what Paul was saying in Philippians 3:13. He had a lot to rest on that was comfortable. He had his education. He had his theological pedigree. He had his affluence and influence. All of those things were in his past. They represented his old level. How does he respond? He chooses to forget what was in the background and presses and reaches and pushes into the things which are ahead.

This is the key to breaking the old cycles associated with the old season—simply starting new ones.

When you step out of your comfort zone, you will learn how to navigate in your new season.

For so many people, comfort is an idol. It's only when you step out of your comfort zone that you can start learning how to navigate the unfamiliar terrain of your new season. Paul was a Pharisee turned preacher of the Gospel. He was an academic turned traveling evangelist. He was ushered into a dimension of living he had never conceived of, and yet he preferred to press toward the glorious unknown than choose to rest in his pampered past. He knew what was ahead was greater than what was behind.

I pray that this releases a stirring in your spirit that what's in your future, what's ahead and on the horizon is overwhelmingly superior to what was behind, even if what was behind appeared to be a benchmark.

Too many of us get stuck in old cycles because we put limits on God. We limit what He can do with our potential. We think that the old life and all its trimmings was as good as it gets. God wants to bust apart your idea of what "as good as it gets" looks like. You haven't dreamed of what God can do. You can't comprehend what's up ahead. Your mind cannot begin to fathom what the Almighty has on the other side of your new season.

I declare to you, according to the Word of God, that *"Eye has not seen, nor ear heard, nor have entered into the heart of man the things which God has prepared for those who love Him"* (1 Corinthians 2:9). That statement alone is grounds for a shout, but don't stop there.

We look at verses like this, get a spiritual high, and then settle right back in to our old cycles. Why? Because we isolate ourselves from the incomparable, unimaginable things God wants to bring into our lives. This verse wows us, showing what God wants to do, and yes, even has prepared *"for those who love Him,"* but look at what Paul adds in the following verse— *"But God has revealed them to us through His Spirit"* (v. 10).

Okay, now it's time to shout! Why? Because right here we discover that even though we're stepping into new dimensions, there is a promise that we will *not* always have to walk in the dark. The Spirit of the living God dwells inside you. The One who searches and knows the mind of God, the deep things of His heart, dwells in you and tells you where to go (see 1 Corinthians 2:10-12, 3:16; John 16:13). He directs your footsteps. He gives you wisdom. He releases understanding. He brings clarity. You have not been left alone as an orphan—God Himself has come to live inside you in the Person of the Holy Spirit (see John 14:18).

Yes, you will walk through the dark, but you will not walk through the dark of a new season alone because God is always with you. God is in you. God is for you. God is in your corner.

I believe the Lord is saying to you, "The cycle has been broken over your life!" It's completely broken. You're never going to be the same. How you used to do things won't define how you do them in your next dimension. You're going to speak differently. You're going to stand differently. You're going to teach differently. You're going to run numbers differently. You're going to sing differently. You're going to practice medicine differently. You're going to raise your kids differently. You're going to love your spouse differently. Everything's different because it's a new dimension!

Reflection Questions

1. What's the difference between *doing* and *becoming?*

2. How is it a good thing to be the "low person at a new level"?

3. Describe what it looks like to *walk in the dark*. How have you experienced this in your life?

CHAPTER 7

THE FINAL TESTS

And he [Elijah] *said to him, "Go back again, for what have I done to you?"* (1 Kings 19:20).

In this last chapter, I want to arm you with some practical tools to help you identify whether or not you are living in alignment with your new level. When you get there, you need to stay there. Remember, you're changed. You're a new man. A new woman. Elisha *became* Elijah's servant. One of the worst things that we can experience is living out of alignment with our new level. Why? It produces purposeless-ness. You will always be making strides toward fulfilling your purpose as you live in alignment with your level.

Here are some simple tests that will help you recognize whether or not you are living on par with the place that power promoted you into.

THE ROOM TEST

First, we have the *room test*. I always say that if you are the smartest person in a room, you are in the wrong room. Get out! You are too big for that room. Think about it for a minute. If you are going to live at another level, you need to always be learning. You need to always be progressing. There's always something to read. There's always a seminar to watch or listen to. There's always room for development. I'm not saying to become a workaholic. What I am inviting you into is a process. Process means there is room to grow.

> **If you are the smartest person in a room, you are in the wrong room. Get out!**

Elisha might have been the smartest guy in town—or at least the smartest when it came to what he knew. But everything changed when Elijah came by. The master plower was touched by the master prophet, and now the guy's whole identity shifted. The master quickly became the apprentice. This is truly the test of whether or not you are living in alignment with your new level. If you seek out places where you are the smartest person in the room, you need to find some new rooms. Seek out some different influences. Find people who challenge you and draw out your potential.

THE WOMB TEST

> [Jesus said], *"Most assuredly, I say to you, unless one is born again, he cannot see the kingdom of God"* (John 3:3).

Second is the *womb test*. If you want to *see* at a new level, you're going to have to be born again. In the same way you needed to experience a birthing process to see the Kingdom of God, you need to be born in order to see your new dimension of living.

We're going to stay here a little bit longer, as I believe if you truly get this, you will never try to squeeze back into an old season again.

If where you currently are can't fit you anymore, you need to be born. You need to come out. It's like a mother who is ready to give birth. I believe this is where you were when power passed by. Elisha was ready for transition, and all it took was a push from Elijah to turn the plowman into a prophet in training.

The womb got too small to hold you, and you needed to come out. You needed to make a transition from the womb to the room. You needed to get out of a small place and step into a larger place. You might have been the largest person in that womb, but now, on the outside, you feel like the smallest person in the new world. That means you've graduated to a new level. Now it's time for you to grow. It's time to develop. It's time to learn how to say "Ma-Ma" and "Da-Da."

That womb is too small to hold you. You've outgrown it, and the discomfort is between the womb and the infant. It's painful to the mother and it's painful to the baby when you've outgrown the space you've been in. The only choice you have is to be born. Your only option is to come out. This is what happened when power met potential, and Elijah gave Elisha his mantle. That was the push Elisha's potential needed in order to come forth.

Can you imagine if, along the way, Elisha turned and tried to go back to his old way of living? Sometimes that happens. Even though we've been born, and we have become a new person at a new level, we can get distracted by old level stuff. Old level situations. Old level places. Old level people. Old level activities. We try to participate, but they hurt. Why? It's like a two year old trying to go back into the mother's womb. It's just painful. It just doesn't work. It just doesn't look right. It makes no sense. The baby doesn't belong there.

How are you feeling right now?

YOU ARE BREAKING OUT

Are there things in your life trying to squeeze you back into your former level? It won't work. It can't. You're new. Elisha was a prophet, not a plowman. You're a new person on a new course living at a new level. If you feel the strain and the pain of being pushed back into the womb, get out of those situations. That's not where you belong.

The same was true for Nicodemus in John 3. The man was not like the Sanhedrin court that he came from. You are not like your background. How do I know you're not one of *them?* Because you see on a whole different level. Nicodemus perceived something about this

Man Jesus that none of his colleagues and peers were pressing into. Nicodemus was in transition. He recognized something about Jesus that his cohorts did not understand. He could not convince them because he has been birthed into a new dimension, and they were still operating at the old one.

> *You're a new person on a new course living at a new level.*

It was time for the teacher to become a student again. Nicodemus was *"a ruler of the Jews"* (John 3:1). He was a leader and an authority. He had power and position. His old level was full of prestige among his people. But there was a problem—the water had broken over his life. He met power. Something was happening inside him. He started to see at a new level.

I want to announce to you that the water has broken over your life. You will have to be fed on another level. You're not going to get nourishment through the cord from which you used to receive food. You're going to have to take more responsibility for your food. You cannot just live from sermon to sermon.

In the past, the Lord fed you manna falling down into your tent, but now you're coming into your promised land. Prepare your victuals; for in three days you will cross this Jordan. You are coming into another dimension. You've got to begin to feed on another level. Learn on another level. Read on another level. Interact with people on another level. Parent on another level. Run a household on another level. Build a business on another level. Treat patients on another level. Everything is upgraded.

You have got to get out of that womb. And if you're already out, don't go back there. Don't be drawn back to a place that won't fit you. Don't be enticed by those rooms where you are the know-it-all. Deep down, you know you've got to get out. You've got to get out of this rut.

You've got to get rid of that plow. You've got to burn the ox.

POTENTIAL'S FINAL TEST

Potential, here is your final test. Elijah says to Elisha, *"Go back home."* We've looked at that process already, where Elisha returns home, deals with the townsmen, prepares them a meal, burns his plow, and moves onward. We've already gone through all of that.

Now I want us to look at the test of discouragement. This is the last test Elisha needs to pass before he moves forward.

> *You cannot earn the right to lead until you pass the test of discouragement.*

You cannot earn the right to lead until you pass the test of discouragement. If I can talk you out of it, you are not the one. Elijah tried out this test on Elisha to see what he was made of, to see if he really was the one. Yes, he caught the mantle. Yes, he ran up to Elijah. Obviously, he knew he got something. He recognized that power touched something.

Here is the true test. Will your realized potential survive discouragement? Look at how Elijah responded to the excited Elisha. He looked at him and said, *"Go back again, for what have I done to you?"* (1 Kings 19:20). This wasn't nice. It did not sound affirming at first. The one who brought power that unlocked potential was now telling Elisha to go back home.

More than anything, Elijah was looking to see how Elisha would respond. Would he get bent out of shape? Would he go home and not return? Would Elijah's harsh attitude push the plowman away? How much did Elisha really want his new level? The test was issued. How would Elisha respond?

How will you respond?

Will you keep moving forward if things don't unfold the way you think they should? Will you keep following even if you get offended?

Upset? If someone talks to you the wrong way? If someone corrects you? If somebody criticizes you? If others point fingers and laugh at you? Will you keep moving forward if you forget why you were doing this to begin with? *What got into me? Why am I going in this direction? I can't see at this new level. It's all alien. It's all unfamiliar. At least in the old level I knew where everything was. I knew how everything worked. Everything made sense.*

What will you follow? These thoughts are not unusual; they aren't bad. They're normal. They are the common assaults upon everyone who is invited into a new dimension.

The test is passed or failed in how you *respond* to the thoughts and feelings and temptations and persecutions and offenses. You don't fail if you feel. You don't fail if you think. You don't fail if you catch yourself asking why. You don't fail if your mind starts trying to make sense of what you're doing and where you're going. These things don't determine your grade.

It's what you do that determines where you go. The next level has to be that real to you. That necessary. It's got to become so real to you that you can't breathe without it.

THE NEXT BREATH TEST

A young preacher saw an old retired preacher who had a massive, huge, anointed ministry. The old preacher was fishing down by the riverbed. This young preacher approached the old preacher and said to him, "I hate to bother you, but this is my opportunity. I may never get this chance again, and I want to minister under the same kind of glory that you minister under."

The old man didn't even look up at him. He kept on fishing. The young preacher started to walk away, and he thought to himself, *I may never have this chance again.* He said, "Mr., I hate to bother you, but I can't walk away. I may never get this chance again, and I want to minister under the same anointing under which you minister."

So the old man kept on fishing. And the young man kept bothering him and bothering him and bothering him. Finally, the old man put down the fishing rod, got up on his feet and snatched the young guy by his neck. He picked him up and threw him into the water. The guy couldn't swim. He couldn't swim in that dimension, so he started going down in it and coming up again. "Help!" he cried. He went down in the water again, and then popped back up, "Help!" Up and down he went, all the while crying out for help.

Finally, the old man reached down into the water, stretched forth his hand, and snatched him out of the water. The young preacher was panting. He was gasping for air. He was confused and crying. "But I don't understand. I respected you. I admired you, and you pick me up and throw me into the water. I can't swim."

The old man looked at him and said, "You remember that last time you came up out of the water?" The young man was still catching his breath, "Of course I remember. I can't forget it." He said, "You remember how badly you wanted that next breath?" He said, "Of course I remember. If I didn't get another breath, I was going to die." The old preacher said, "That's how badly you have to want it. You have to want it like you want your last breath. When you want it like that, then you're ready."

You've got to walk into that next level like you need your next breath of air. You're not playing with it. It's not some game. When you want purpose bad enough to do whatever it takes to get there—to control your passions, your foolishness, and your craziness to get there—that's when you're ready to step into it.

Purpose awaits the ready. God's not playing hide-and-seek with your purpose. He's looking for those who are actually serious about stepping into what they've been designed to do.

When you're ready to stay up and study while other people play games to get there, then you're ready. Nobody's going to give you purpose on credit. Nobody's going to give it to you because you look cute. You have to pay the price to operate in the next dimension, and after you've suffered awhile, and after you've been talked about a while, and after you've faced all kinds of discouragement and come through all kinds of hell and say, "I still want it," then God says, "I'm going to release another wave of glory in your life."

> *God's not playing hide-and-seek with your purpose. He's looking for those who are serious about stepping into their destiny.*

If you want it, you've got to run. Not walk. Not slug. Not wade. Not shuffle. Not jig. Not dance. You've got to run into it and run with it. Elisha got the mantle and ran toward Elijah. He could have gotten discouraged when

Elijah told him to go back. But he didn't. He thought, *Go back...to what? I've got nothing to go back to. I've been ruined and wrecked for anything I could possibly go back to. Forward's the only option. That's the only route I want to travel.*

The pace has changed. You might have been thrown in the water several times. You almost drowned several times. You nearly died several times. You almost went completely under—but there was something down inside that kept you fighting your way back up again.

Because of your potential, because of the purpose you've been marked for, God did not let the waters drown you. He said, *"When you pass through the waters, I will be with you; and through the rivers, they shall not overflow you. When you walk through the fire, you shall not be burned, nor shall the flame scorch you. For I am the Lord your God..."* (Isaiah 43:2-3).

The Lord your God is with you. He was with you through the past, He is with you in the present, and He will be with you for the future.

He's not leaving or moving, for He says, *"For I am the Lord, I do not change..."* (Malachi 3:6).

Anybody else would have drowned in the hell you went through. Anybody else would have died in it. Anybody else would have lost their mind. Anybody else would have had a nervous breakdown, but you kept fighting your way back up to the top. And now there is a glory that God is going to release on your life.

Don't be mistaken, it has to be released on the *extraordinary*. Not the perfect. Not the all-cleaned-up. Not the goodie-two-shoes. Extraordinary is the one willing to do whatever it takes to walk in the new dimension.

> **Your purpose fulfilled releases solutions to the world.**

It cannot be released on somebody who hasn't been over their head, almost gone under, nearly collapsed, almost fainted, and almost lost their mind. You are the future. Your purpose fulfilled releases solutions to this world. A double portion is at your disposal. Just when you thought you had it all, God says, "I'm taking you higher. I'm about to blow your mind."

If you thought your last level was the best, I've got good news for you—your eye has not seen, nor has your ear heard, nor has your heart even imagined what God is unlocking in your life!

Reflection Questions

1. What is the room test? The womb test?

2. How have you experienced either one of these tests in your life? What did they look like?

3. What does the next breath test look like to you? How have you experienced this one?

CONCLUSION

Then the hand of the Lord came upon Elijah...
(1 Kings 18:46).

Now to Him who is able to do exceedingly abundantly above all that we ask or think, according to the power that works in us (Ephesians 3:20).

In our final moments together, I don't want you to just close this book, put it on the shelf, and go back to living life as usual. I hope you received some good information; but most of all, I want to see you experience an impartation.

I want these pages to serve as your escort into the next level, your new dimension. I pray the Spirit of God whetted your appetite for new realms of glory, anointing, potential, and power that you didn't even know were inside of you. They were just waiting to be unlocked by those destiny-defining collisions.

So here is my prayer for you—that the powerful hand of the Lord would come upon you, even now while you read these words. As the hand of the Lord was upon Elijah, and the hand of the Lord was upon Elisha, I pray that you experience this same touch of power that unlocks your new dimension and launches you into new levels of living.

I pray that the powerful hand of the Lord would be upon every area of your life. Not one gift or talent remains untouched by His grace. Not one ounce of potential misses out. The hand of the Lord is upon your house. The hand of the Lord is upon your business. The hand of the Lord is upon your ministry. The hand of the

Lord is on your family. The hand of the Lord is on your schooling. The hand of the Lord is on your finances. The hand of the Lord is on your past. The hand of the Lord is on your debts. The hand of the Lord is upon *you*.

So let this be your prayer:

> *Lord, whatever You're doing in the earth right now, don't do it without me. Touch me with Your power and unlock the potential, the gifts, the talents, and the abilities within me. Orchestrate those destiny-defining appointments. Give me eyes to see what You're doing. Ears to hear You speaking. And a heart that responds to how You're moving in my life. I run toward everything You have for me, not looking back. Thank You, Father, for unlocking my purpose for Your glory in Jesus's name!*

Paralyzed? Loose Yourself!

Ask, and it will be given to you;
seek, and you will find; Knock,
and it will be opened to you.

—Matthew 7:7

After we know the dream God wants for our lives, what do we do after that?

At times we can become frozen in desire. It's like we're paralyzed and can't move forward. Often times we are locked in position because we are not able to speak. This is because we have made ourselves believe that we have no power, but the reality is that the power to be free from the dead things comes from within you.

Labels can deplete your power and paralyze you! You don't have to live by the labels that others place on you—you can live by the labels you speak on yourself.

Has someone told you that your dream is impossible? If you internalize his negativity and make that your belief, then you will stop pursuing your gift and progress will be stopped. Believe in yourself and speak life over yourself; otherwise, you will remain in the chains that others spoke on you, and you will not be able to loose yourself.

Labels can deplete your power
and paralyze you!

Loose Yourself from Lies

So here it is! Are you ready for your first challenge in this chapter? I challenge you to stop living by what others said about you, and start speaking God's thoughts over yourself. Don't cry out to people, cry out to God.

Often times we are paralyzed and unable to get the things we desire because we haven't spoken for ourselves. We haven't believed the power of life and death is in our tongue.

I am the children's ministry director of The Potter's House Church of Dallas now, but when I started I was not the director. I walked into the office with the desire for something bigger than the position I was in; but just as this book says, I had to go through a process. I had to evaluate my support system. I had to start faithing it, and I had to speak it.

Don't cry out to people, cry out to God.

So when I walked into the office, I spoke, "I will be the director of this ministry as I have seen it in visions that have been given to me, according to God's perfect will and timing." I wasn't the director at the time that I spoke it, but I am the director now. What would have happened if I didn't speak it? I would still be in a mediocre position, receiving mediocre praises and getting mediocre pay, when God called me to a bigger position than that. I had to speak what I wanted and accept and go through the process so that I could produce my purpose. Your purpose, power, and promise cannot be obtained without you opening your mouth to speak what you see. Speak out and loose yourself!

As the director, I find that our children believe that they are whatever you speak. So I hear kids tell me:

I'm bad.

I have anger issues.

I can't do this.

The children truly believe these lies! So often children don't produce life because their parents don't speak life to them. So how does that pertain to who we are now? Whatever was spoken on you as a child will stay with you into adulthood. If your parents spoke life over you, then you experience more freedom than most. If your parents neglected to speak life, then you likely feel paralyzed in certain areas because you believe what they said all those years ago is actually true. We have to loose ourselves from those lies! For the Bible says this:

> *People of Zion, who live in Jerusalem, you will weep no more. How gracious He will be when you cry for help! As soon as He hears, He will answer you* (Isaiah 30:19 NIV).

God will answer you and be gracious if He HEARS YOU, but God can't hear your cry unless HE HEARS YOUR CRY!

If you don't believe in your dream, no one else will. If you don't believe you have a world-changing purpose, then you won't change the world. Instead, you will be swallowed up by the world that you were supposed to change! Why? Because you were too busy living in what somebody else said. Speak what God's shown you. Speak what you see and desire. If you don't speak up for yourself, then you will be submerged in the bottom of the barrel watching others take the world by storm. You don't want to sit, as the lame man did, on the side of the pool, letting people step over you to gain something that could have easily been yours, had you wanted it badly enough.

Loose Yourself from Worry

I want to talk to you for a moment about work over worry. Sometimes we can allow ourselves to be consumed by the worry of the timing of our promise, purpose, and power. We become worried about the "when" factor—*when* is God going to make it happen. Worry will rob us of our joy, our peace, and our dream.

Faithing it will take you over the temptation of worry. Let me explain.

You should not worry about when God is going to lift you out of your process and into your purpose. Just stay focused on your work at hand. Faith without works is dead—that's what the Word says! That simply means you have to work for what you believe God for.

My mother-in-law use to always say, if you are going pray, don't worry. If you are going to worry, don't pray. I love that saying because often times we will pray for something from God but not put effort into the work at hand. So far we've learned that everything you desire to obtain from God is given after you do something. So if you have asked God for something but you are not seeing it manifest, perhaps instead of thinking it's the devil, a spirit, or that you need to fast, perhaps you need to go to work. If you want to see the fruits of your labor, you have to do the work to plant the seed.

> *If you are going pray, don't worry. If you are going to worry, don't pray.*

Loose Yourself from Laziness

Asking God (prayer) isn't going to get a field planted. You have to go out there and plant the seeds. If you don't, you will look at your surroundings and everyone's field is producing but yours. In that case, you cannot be upset if the people around you sowed and did the work and they are seeing a harvest, but your field is empty. If you are not willing to sow, then you will not reap. We can stand in our seedless field and worry why it's not growing. In fact, we worry instead of spending our time planting seeds into the field. If you don't want to work, then don't speak, don't ask, and don't knock. Everything you believe God for is going to come with some work, and if you don't want to work really hard to produce a big harvest, then you should not ask for a big purpose. You will receive a big harvest when you are willing to work hard. The people you see being blessed are receiving an overflow blessing because they out put an overflow of seeds. Do not be jealous of others who are reaping more! Rather, question what you have sown.

The problem is we often ask for more from God than we are willing to work for or give. So yes, we can worry about the harvest that we aren't receiving, or we can do something else. So here it is—I am giving you another challenge: I challenge you to match the amount of harvest you want to the amount of work you'll do. Then do as my mother-in-law says. If you are going to pray, don't worry, and if you are going to worry, don't pray.

Jealousy is deadly to the soul, and it will stop you from moving forward. It's important that you stop worrying about other people's things and blessings, and start working on yourself. A big part of declaring your promise is the understanding that even in declaring what you want you have to put in work. Yes, we want to pray, declare, and decree, but you also have to put in work when you want to obtain anything.

You and I have to put in time at our jobs in order to receive a paycheck. In a relationship, we put in work in order to be fruitful and multiply.

Nothing is just handed to you—it is received through hard work.

Loose Yourself from the Past

We all have gone through something that makes us angry and shakes our faith. If we didn't go through something to shake our faith, then God would have never said that faith the size of a mustard seed can move the mountain. Things will shake your faith, but those things have come to bring about the strength in you.

All you have to do is press forward. Stop thinking about why He allowed the rape, molestation, abuse, divorce, abortion, fornication, pregnancy, and so on to happen. Start using the things you overcame to help you declare what is rightfully yours. If you don't go through anything, then you have nothing to talk about. If you have nothing to talk about, then what are you going to ask God for? The power to obtain your promise is based on your ability to embrace the process of the pain.

I know what it's like to be hurt, to be broken, to be bitter, and to be angry. But I decided to speak life to myself and to loose myself from the things that were hindering me. You may have been beaten and you may feel broken, bitter, angry, and hurt, but God has not forgotten about you. You will overcome this! It's time to speak life, and speak out.

When you can speak out about what you've overcome, then the enemy can't use it over you anymore. Your broken self, your bitter self, your negative emotions take power from you. Faith leaves, negativity enters, and you are hindered.

God may have taken you through the storm, but He still gave you a rainbow, and the point is He took you through it. Start looking at your low points as an opportunity for God to show you His power to bring you out. You will not remain paralyzed at this low point forever! Don't allow your hurt to hinder you from reaching for power, let it motivate you to search for a healer. My dear friend, I speak to you and I say to you without hesitation, "You can heal while hurting."

Gain back your power! Overcome the things that are hindering you. When you are able to climb over the rape, the abuse, the humiliation, the embarrassment, the lies, and the hurt then you will step into your promise.

Loose Yourself from Failure Feelings

I have seen God show up for me even when I didn't deserve it. I believe that you can still be elevated to a high level in Christ even if you don't feel you deserve it. I also believe that the people who stay in that humble vein are the ones who receive the most promotion. It's the people who are willing to withstand the fire that are met by God and then promoted.

Just think about Shadrach, Meshach, and Abednego. They were willing to go into the fire for God because they had faith He would save them. They received great promotion after they withstood the fire, and they were just doing what they felt God would have them to do. God brought them to high promotion because they remained humble and low in spirit (see Daniel 1–3). Your humility will open the doors that pride will close. Moses didn't believe He deserved it; but he stayed humble, and God used Him, and God can still use you.

No matter what happened to you, no matter what you went through, God can use you. You don't have to be whole in order for God to use and answer what you declare.

*It's the people who are willing to
withstand the fire that are met
by God and then promoted.*

We allow the people who hurt us to take our power, and then we get upset when we are standing powerless, paralyzed, and without direction. Take your power back! Start declaring death on some things and speaking life on other things. What would happen if you were one declaration away from receiving your deliverance? What if all you had to do was speak death on that soul tie, speak death on that sickness, speak death on that past hurt, speak death on that past relationship, and start speaking life on your situation and your circumstance.

God can't bless you if you don't open your mouth. You must first be willing to let go of the weight that is keeping you from leaping into your perfect purpose.

To the people that didn't believe in you? Prove them wrong. You deserve to be at the top of the mountain, just don't get too busy concentrating on the people who have hurt you or surpassed you. Focus on where you are now and work to make it to the top. I am behind you!

I want you to know that you can reach the top.

I want you to know that you do have a gift.

I want you to know that you are talented and necessary in the Kingdom.

> *God can't bless you if you*
> *don't open your mouth.*

Prayer—Get Real with God

Prayer got me out of my situation. I found true freedom when I communicated with God.

I was real, open, and vulnerable with the only person who knows everything about me today, and everything about where I am going. Prayer allowed me the opportunity to talk to God—to speak to Him, to tell Him about my hurt, my pain, and my anger. If you can't be real with God about the things that hurt you and anger you, then you aren't having a real relationship. We always get in this stigma of saying you aren't supposed to ask God why. I don't know why we tell people that, because when Jesus was suspended on the cross, pierced in his hands and feet, he looked up at His Father and said something. The Bible says in Mark 15:34, *"And at three in the afternoon Jesus cried out in a loud voice, 'Eloi, Eloi, lema sabachthani?'* (which means 'My God, my God, why have you forsaken me?')" (NIV).

Jesus was in relationship with God His Father. He felt connected to Him, and we too should have the same connection. God is your

Father. If you don't know what's going on, if you want to ask your Daddy a question, then you ask Him. Don't sit in your anger and bitterness because you are afraid to ask God why. It is through our inability to connect with God in communication that the enemy is able to destroy us. Take your true self to God without hesitation! Go to Him in spirit and in truth, then you will have a breakthrough that will change your life for the better.

You deserve to have a relationship with your Father God. And if you know God better, in turn, you will know you better. In fact, this is how you tap into the thing that makes you royalty! The God that healed the blind, raised the dead, and turned water into wine is the same miracle-working God in you. Also, while you're talking to your Father, ask Him for a strategy to help you produce your purpose. It takes more than just speaking it as you know, but you also need strategy you need a plan and you then need to walk it out.

You can get your power back! Go before the Lord with your anger, and allow Him to heal you so that you are able to push forward in what He has for you.

Write a Letter to God

Are you carrying your cross and going through turmoil? Do you feel beaten and crushed? Even paralyzed? This is the perfect time to look to Him.

This is what I want you to do. I want you to write a letter to God asking Him, "Why?" But listen to me, I want you to ask Him why from your hurt and broken place. When I went before God with my why it was, "Why would You make me go through infertility? Why would You allow them to hurt me?" I had several why's but I ended my letter telling God my truth. This was my truth to Him: "God I'm hurting and I'm angry. I love You and I want to trust You, but I am scared, and I need to know why I had to go through all this beating and all this crushing? I know You love me more than this, Lord. Help me to have faith in Your ability to give me everything I'm believing You for, even though I am hurt from what You allowed me to endure."

I received my answer, and I'm praying you will receive yours as well. God has a strategy and a plan for you, but you can't have access to the room until you are willing to address your situation.

What Am I Talking About?

God created the world all from the words that came from His mouth. God showed us that in order for us to produce greatness we must connect to the power that we have in our mouths. We can obtain whatever we speak while in relationship with God! How do I know? The Bible tells me so!

> *Ask and it will be given to you; seek and you will find; knock and the door will be opened to you* (Matthew 7:7 NIV).

We sometimes allow ourselves to stay in bondage and not have what is rightfully ours. All of this bondage is unnecessary. Speak to the mountain. Ask. Seek. Knock. If you want to obtain the thing that God has for you, speak it out. You have no more excuses! We have reached the point of knowing that you have to speak what you want to produce.

Ask and receive. Your purpose is of no value if it isn't spoken for. A lot of us have promises and purposes waiting for us, but we are unable to obtain them because we simply haven't opened our mouths. We haven't knocked on the door. We haven't declared our promise to come forth. So, what are you talking about? Are you wasting your words on something besides your God-given dream?

Everything that unlocks our blessings comes from our mouths. Let's look at another Scripture:

> *Again, truly I tell you that if two of you on earth agree about anything they ask for, it will be done for them by my Father in Heaven* (Matthew 18:19 NIV).

To *ask* means "to say something in order to obtain an answer or some information." There it is again—*say something*. If you don't speak, you can't obtain. If you allow yourself to be tongue-tied by the webs of the enemy, you will stay paralyzed—and you can't be upset when you don't have what is rightfully yours. Speak out! Don't allow people to speak for you. Speak for yourself. Part of bringing purpose back to life is to speak life.

Are you wasting your words on something besides your God-given dream?

Declare your promise, declare your power, and loose yourself from the entanglements of the world. Start labeling yourself according to what God thinks about you. Open your mouth so you can obtain your victory, promise, and power. It's in your mouth! Victory is in your mouth. If you don't decree and declare your vision then it can't come to pass. In this moment you must understand that you are a child of the King; therefore, you have rights to Kingdom blessings. But you must go through the pain of the process and embrace it and start declaring things over yourself.

You are linked to greatness—Jesus Christ. Therefore, you deserve greatness, but not without great struggles. Be delivered from your pain. Speak over yourself, address yourself, gain real relationship with Christ, and leap into your destiny and walk it out.

I Tell You, ARISE

I am speaking to the scared you that is afraid to speak life because of the fear of what your success looks like in God's eyes. I speak to you, and I tell you, "Arise, my king, queen, prince, princess. Arise. You were born to be great. You are an heir to the King of kings. You have a lot to offer, and you have a lot to give. You can do it. Pursue your dream. Press through. Whatever you do, don't let failure stop you—let it push you. Whatever you do, don't let downfalls keep you from going up the hill. You are royalty, you own the light, and you choose whether you will rest in the light or settle in the darkness. So

I take this time to speak and declare life over your purpose and your promise."

You are royalty, you own the light.

I pray that God places a heart in you that seeks Him with all that you have. I pray that God ignites the power within you to bring forth the things that He has spoken over your life. I pray that God restores you from the pain that you allowed to consume you. I pray God removes the weight that hinders you from being able to leap into your purpose. I pray that the pain of the past not be an issue for you, but that you use the past pains to press you forward. I pray that God would break every generational curse that you have accepted and that which you haven't accepted that has tried to bind you, and we curse it at the root. I pray that the fire of God seals every area of your life that is aligned with His perfect will and purpose for you. I pray that you would press forward and begin to speak life to the areas that need to be brought back to life and speak death to the bad areas that need to be dead. You are to be great in your purpose! I pray you begin to open your mouth and work and that the minute you do, your harvest be plentiful and overflowing. I thank God that you are walking into your purpose with power, and that you are faithing it from the day forward. Thank you God, it is so and so it is. Amen!

You are royalty, you own the light.

STRENGTH
FOR EVERY
MOMENT

DAY 1
I CAN DO ALL THINGS

I can do all things through Christ who strengthens me (Philippians 4:13).

ECEPTION is a trap and stronghold that ensnares many, especially those not content with their own present state in life. The Bible instructs us that we must learn to be content in whatever state we find ourselves. The apostle Paul learned that lesson well: "*...for I have learned, in whatsoever state I am, therewith to be content*" (Phil. 4:11 KJV).

This is not to imply that we should be satisfied with being bound by the devil or be content with complacency and mediocrity, thus not fulfilling the call of God on our lives. Not at all. We are to work to improve ourselves while at the same time remaining totally dependent on God.

Self-sufficiency means to be "sufficient in oneself" and not putting your faith in God's assistance. Contentment, on the other hand, is to know with certainty and absolute firm conviction that God is able to meet your every need; Jehovah is your all-sufficiency. Contentment means that you are aware that you don't covet another person's position, property, possessions, or personality. Why? Because you know and are assured that all you presently have and all that you are today is more than enough in the hands of God. Whatever you need to do to fulfill God's purpose you can do, not in your own strength, but through the strength and power of Christ that dwells within your innermost being.

The apostle Paul said:

I know how to be abased, and I know how to abound. Everywhere and in all things I have learned both to be full and to be hungry, both to abound and to suffer need. I can do all things through Christ who strengthens me (Phil. 4:12-13).

CONSIDERATIONS

1. Like Paul, have you learned to be content in your present state in life? Why or why not? What possible ways are you being deceived into discontentment?

   _____

   _____

   _____

2. In your own words, define the difference between being content and being complacent. Are you doing all you can do to fulfill the call of God in your life?

   _____

   _____

11

3. List five things that you think of when you consider the word "contentment." Are those things present in your life? How can you improve your contentment level?

_____

_____

_____

_____

_____

4. Contentment means that you don't covet another person's position, property, possessions, or personality. Was there a time (or times) when you were aware of coveting another's position, property, possessions, or personality? Have you completely abandoned those thoughts and desires? Why or why not?

_____

_____

_____

5. What recent steps have you taken to fulfill God's purpose for you? What additional steps can you take today, tomorrow?

_____

_____

_____

_____

MEDITATION

I know how to be abased, and I know how to abound. Everywhere and in all things I have learned both to be full and to be hungry, both to abound and to suffer need. I can do all things through Christ who strengthens me (Philippians 4:12-13).

Do you trust Christ to give you strength to do *all* things?

Day 2
Renew Your Strength

*He gives power to the weak, and to those who have no might He increases strength. Even the youths shall faint and be weary, and the young men shall utterly fall, but those who wait on the Lord shall **renew their strength**; they shall mount up with wings like eagles, they shall run and not be weary, they shall walk and not faint* (Isaiah 40:29-31).

When your pity party is over and you are ready for His help, God will say, "Don't you know? Have you not heard Who I am—the everlasting God? I am the Creator of the universe. I am not a child; I am not a school boy—I am God. Who do you think you're fooling? I'm God. I hold your breath in My hands. I created your body. I heat your blood just hot enough to keep you alive but not so hot that you die. Who else do you allow to control your life? If it is not Me, then who? I love you. I created you in My image. I am that I am."

What more does the Lord have to do or say to show you He loves you? Don't let satan continue to fool you into thinking that God has forsaken you.

Stop doing things that you know you don't have any business doing. Repent and confess your sins instead of spending your time pointing out the sins of everyone else. Admit that you have fallen so that your healing may begin.

CONSIDERATIONS

1. Have you hosted your own pity party lately? Did you invite others? How do you feel after the party is over? Refreshed or defeated?

   _____

   _____

   _____

2. Do you believe that God is the great "I am"? What does that title or term mean to you? Define the great "I am" in two to three sentences.

   _____

   _____

   _____

   _____

3. Think of 10 ways that the Lord helps you through each day. Write them down and thank Him for each one.

_____

_____

_____

_____

_____

4. Has satan fooled you into thinking that God has forsaken you? What can you do to keep satan from fooling you?

_____

_____

5. Most people tend to judge others but don't realize the things wrong in their own lives. The next time you start to say something about another, stop first and think about issues in your own life that need to be addressed.

MEDITATION

*He gives power to the weak, and to those who have no might He increases strength. Even the youths shall faint and be weary, and the young men shall utterly fall, but those who wait on the Lord shall **renew their strength**; they shall mount up with wings like eagles, they shall run and not be weary, they shall walk and not faint* (Isaiah 40:29-31).

How many times have you felt faint and weak, but the Lord renewed your strength and you went on to accomplish your goal?

Day 3
My Understanding Returned

*And at the end of the time I, Nebuchadnezzar, lifted my eyes to Heaven, and **my understanding returned** to me; and I blessed the Most High and praised and honored Him who lives forever…. At the same time my reason returned to me, and for the glory of my kingdom, my honor and splendor returned to me. My counselors and nobles resorted to me, I was restored to my kingdom, and excellent majesty was added to me. Now I, Nebuchadnezzar, praise and extol and honor the King of Heaven, all of whose works are truth, and His ways justice. And those who walk in pride He is able to put down* (Daniel 4:34,36-37).

R epentance was the key to Nebuchadnezzar's healing and deliverance.

To fall is bad enough, but to fall and not cry out for help, refusing to repent for your sin, is worse than the fall itself. Some people are so full of pride and consumed with their own self-sufficiency that they think, "If I can't get up myself, I won't let anyone help me."

Maybe you are ashamed to let anyone know that you have fallen because you don't want them to think less of you. Is your image so important that you're willing to continue in your pitiful fallen state? Are you so deceived that you will not acknowledge that you have sinned? Stop being so proud. After all, isn't that what caused you to fall in the first place?

Pride is dangerous because it forces you to lie needlessly in a helpless state for days—and sometimes years. If you had asked for help immediately, you could have gotten up and gone on with your life.

CONSIDERATIONS

1. *Repent* means to feel remorse, self-reproach, and to feel such regret for past conduct as to change one's mind regarding it. It also means to make a change for the better as a result of contrition for one's sins. Have you repented of conduct that you know God would not approve?

   _____

   _____

2. All are guilty of prideful thoughts and actions from time to time. Think of a time that you know pride was the root of the problem. Did you dig it out and destroy it? If not, do so soon.

   _____

   _____

3. Is it hard for you to ask others or God for help?

_____

Why? _____

_____

_____

4. After you ask God for help, how do you feel? Giving your problems to Him totally brings a peace that passes all understanding. Do you know that?

_____

_____

_____

_____

5. Going on with your life after a fall or failure actually empowers you to do greater things. What greater thing can you begin today?

_____

_____

MEDITATION

*And at the end of the time I, Nebuchadnezzar, lifted
my eyes to Heaven, and **my understanding returned**
to me; and I blessed the Most High and praised and
honored Him who lives forever.... At the same time
my reason returned to me, and for the glory of my
kingdom, my honor and splendor returned to me. My
counselors and nobles resorted to me, I was restored to
my kingdom, and excellent majesty was added to me.
Now I, Nebuchadnezzar, praise and extol and honor
the King of Heaven, all of whose works are truth,
and His ways justice. And those who walk in pride
He is able to put down (Daniel 4:34, 36-37).*

Have you lost your understanding of the Most High?
Open your ears, mind, and heart and allow your understanding
and your reasoning to welcome Him into your entire being.

JOIN *the* CLUB

As a member of the **Love to Read Club,** receive exclusive offers for FREE, 99¢ and $1.99 e-books* every week. Plus, get the **latest news** about upcoming releases from **top authors** like...

T.D. Jakes, Bill Johnson, Cindy Trimm, Jim Stovall, Beni Johnson, Myles Munroe, *and more!*

JOIN NOW at *destinyimage.com/freebooks*

SHARE *this* BOOK

Don't let the impact of this book end with you!
Get a discount when you order 3 or more books.

CALL TO ORDER
1-888-987-7033

destinyimage.com 1-800-722-6774